GUN RUNNING AND THE INDIAN NORTH-WEST FRONTIER

GUN RUNNING AND THE INDIAN NORTH-WEST FRONTIER

ARNOLD KEPPEL

Gian Publishing House

29/6 SHAKTI NAGAR · DELHI-110007 · INDIA

GIAN PUBLISHING HOUSE
29/6 SHAKTI NAGAR, DELHI-110007

First Reprint in India, 1987

*Printed at Goyal Offset Printers, Delhi-110035
and published by Gian Publishing House,
Delhi-110007*

MULES CROSSING THE MARAK IN THE PASS OF FASHAK.

Frontispiece.

CONTENTS

LIST OF ILLUSTRATIONS

SKETCH-MAPS

INTRODUCTORY

OF late the interest of the British public has been centred on the internal problems of the Indian Empire, and chiefly those connected with the Hindu portion of the population. As a result of the alarming wave of sedition that swept over Bengal, accompanied by Brahmanical revivals in the two Presidencies, the affairs of the North-West Frontier, together with the problems connected with the Mahommedan subjects of the King-Emperor, have gradually been relegated to a hazardous obscurity, and have not received the attention they deserved. The crisis on the frontier in the autumn of 1910, as a direct result of the suppression of the arms traffic in the Persian Gulf, has had the effect of switching the limelight once again on to this most interesting quarter. People are at last beginning to realize that if the arming of the Pathan belt continues, a frontier rising in the future will be an affair of infinitely more gravity than heretofore. But in spite of this the operations of the blockading squadron in the Persian Gulf are not sufficiently recognized as an integral part of frontier policy, and have attracted attention more from the hazardous nature of the undertaking than from any bearing that the ultimate suppression of the traffic may have on the tranquillity of the frontier. It is with this object, namely, of emphasizing the connection between the operations of the blockading squadron and the preservation of peace on the Pathan border, that I have ventured on the publication of this book. Though it in no sense aims at bringing the history of the frontier up to date, yet so little has been written on this subject since the publication of Mr. Chirol's "Middle Eastern Question" and Mr. Angus Hamilton's "Afghanistan" (to both of which I am indebted as well for the interest I have felt in the subject as for the information therein contained) that I have thought it worth while to devote a chapter to a précis of the Zakka Khel and Mohmand Expeditions.

But it is not only against the independent tribes that anxiety is felt. For a long while now the attitude of the Amir has given cause for anxious speculation as to the real motives that have actuated his policy. Authorities on the frontier would be puzzled to give a dogmatic answer to the question, "What is the true policy of the Amir?" Many would say that he was honestly anxious to fulfil his treaty obligations with the British, but that he was debarred from doing so in an open manner through fear of the loss of influence with his subjects which would result from the maintenance of too close relations with the Government of India. A smaller number would tell you that this was merely a pretext for a more far-seeing policy which aims at the complete independence of the Afghan kingdom of both Great Britain and Russia. Many circumstances point to the idea that the Amir is contemplating a coup of some sort in the near future. Not least among these is the feverish activity which characterizes the training of the Afghan army. At the review at Agra during his visit to India in January, 1907, the Amir is said to have reviled his Sirdars for having led him to believe in the efficiency of his army as a fighting machine. Turkish officers are now engaged in training the Afghan sepoys; modern guns and ammunition are manufactured in Kabul; great attention is paid to the mobility of the force as a whole, and to the clothing (especially boots) and comfort of the individual soldier. Armed with modern rifles, the Afghan army would no doubt prove a formidable fighting machine in war. But the danger lies in the fact that when the Amir takes it into his head that he is in a position to throw off our control he will probably make the attempt, and though we may be sure of the issue in the end, we shall not escape a lengthy campaign and a vast expenditure of treasure, coupled with the anxiety of seditious risings in India at any moment.

The account of the operations of the Mekran Field Force may have a certain interest, seeing that this corner of the Persian dominions has been so rarely visited by Europeans. But the narrative must necessarily be rather bare of incident, for the cogent reason that "a man armed" is not so likely to be admitted into the family circle of those against whom he is marching, or to see "the little savages at play," as a traveller of more peaceable intentions. On the march to Bint hardly a soul was seen, and what few villages we passed were deserted. It was the same story in Biyaban, though here we had the good-fortune to fall in with the gun-runners, my account of which I hope will compare with the account they gave of themselves.

I am indebted to the *Times* for permission to make use of articles of mine contributed from the scene of the operations, as well as for the one contained in the second half of the chapter on the Autumn Crisis on the Frontier. Much of the subject-matter has been rearranged to suit the lapse of time which has occurred. I am also indebted to the proprietors of the *Onlooker* for permission to reproduce photographs of the expedition, taken by myself, which appeared in that paper.

ARNOLD KEPPEL.

QUIDENDHAM, NORFOLK.
October 7, 1911.

GUN-RUNNING AND THE INDIAN NORTH-WEST FRONTIER

CHAPTER I

PESHAWAR AND THE KHAIBAR PASS

"When the spring-time flushes the desert grass,
Our Kafilas wind through the Khyber Pass.
Lean are the camels, but fat the frails;
Light are the purses, but heavy the bales,
As the snow-bound trade of the North comes down
To the market square of Peshawar Town."

Barrack-Room Ballads.

THE rapidity with which, on the North-West Frontier of India, events develop into a crisis, and the latitude that must in consequence be allowed in dealing with them to the Political Officer in charge on the spot, led to the formation, by Lord Curzon in 1901 of the North-West Frontier Province, out of the trans-Indus districts of the Punjab, under a Chief Commissioner directly in touch with the Government of India in the Foreign Department. A similar scheme had already been formulated and approved by Lord Lytton in 1877, which would have placed the political control of the frontier under the Foreign Department, the internal administration remaining, as before, under the Lieutenant-Governor of the Punjab. The outbreak of the second Afghan War, however, prevented this scheme being carried into effect, and it was not till after the close of the Tirah Campaign that it was again revived under the viceroyalty of Lord Elgin. It remained, nevertheless, to Lord Curzon to point out the weak spot, and to insist on the transfer of both political and administrative departments to the Government of India as the only practical means of insuring a successful grappling with the frontier problem. By this masterstroke of constructive statesmanship Lord Curzon succeeded at one stroke in giving to the affairs of the frontier their proper place and true significance in the foreign policy of the Indian Empire. It was inevitable in a huge district like the Punjab, one of the richest in the whole of India, that the affairs of a few small hill-tribes should receive inadequate if conscientious attention, and that their petitions should be shelved and their legitimate aspirations misunderstood. The Lieutenant-Governor of the Punjab had more than enough to do in superintending the economic development of the district under his care, in staving off the insistent claims of famine, disease, and pestilence; and questions which, owing to the pressure of ordinary administrative routine work, had to be held over to await their turn were found on examination to have assumed such dimensions and to wear such a threatening aspect as to leave nothing to be done but to entrust the matter to the tender mercies of the Punjab Frontier Force. Moreover, the Lieutenant-Governor of the Punjab might be an Indian civilian, with Indian civilian modes of thought, and the politics of the frontier might be to him the merest Greek. The task of coping with the innumerable little pitfalls of Pathan or Afghan statecraft requires a more than usually firm grasp of the working of the Pathan or Afghan mind, and more than a nodding acquaintance with the broad lines of frontier policy. Never did the personal equation enter more into the successful management of the people of India than it does with the wild and lawless tribes of the Afghan marches—wild and lawless through sheer wanton savagery, but capable of being schooled and led little by little and step by step into the paths of righteousness by a firm hand, and by the knowledge that their petitions are read and considered by someone who is interested in their welfare, just in his dealings, and, above all, who is in constant personal touch with the headmen, or "maliks," of their tribe.

A mere glance at the map is totally inadequate to convey to the reader the tribal dispositions, the natural divisions, the artificial frontiers, and the character of the country of which the North-West Frontier is made up. In its extraordinary complexity, both politically and geographically, the serrated shark's-tooth line which bisects the province, forming what is known as the "Independent Border," cannot be better understood than by clasping the two hands together and interlacing the fingers, so that those of the right hand may represent the roads running up through independent territory to the British outposts or political agencies at their heads, and the fingers of the left hand the long spurs of mountainous independent territory that run down into the rich level plains of Peshawar and the Derajat. The knuckles of the right hand will then represent the five district centres of Hazara, Peshawar, Kohat, Bannu, and Dera Ismail Khan. In each of these districts settled government exists, and the administration does not differ in essentials from that of other provinces. In independent territory, however, we do not attempt any administration in the ordinary acceptation of the word. No taxes are collected, and justice is meted out, not according to the Indian penal code, but by the "jirga," or assembly of the elders of the tribe. A mass meeting of the elders of the whole of the Afridi tribe, for instance, would correspond very much to the old "Shiremote" of the Saxon heptarchy; and, indeed, there is more in the simile than one would expect at the first glance, for the democratic spirit that is so characteristic a feature in the gradual growth of English customs finds its counterpart in the spirit of liberty and right of free

THE FRONTIER FINGERPOST.

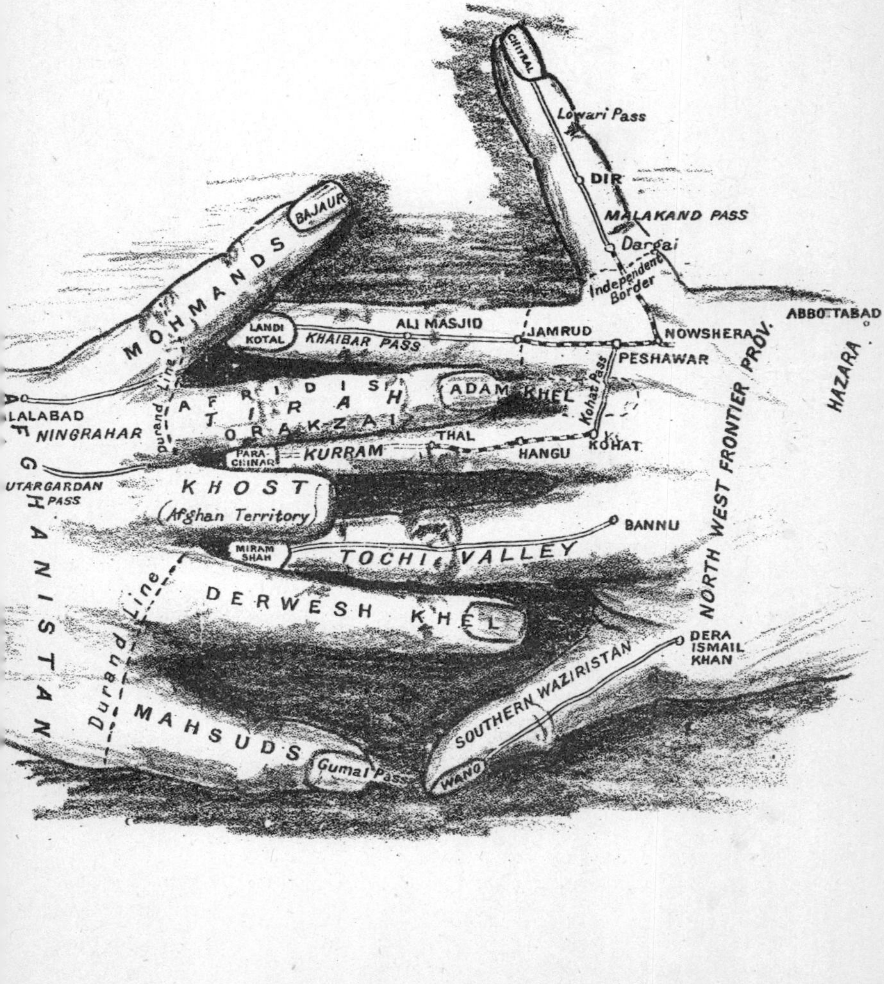

action that is one of the most cherished prerogatives of the Pathan tribesman, be he never so humble. This spirit finds its chief expression in the manly bearing, open countenance, and almost indefinable dignity of this hardy race of hillmen, whose life is one long struggle for the barest existence on the outskirts of a "promised land" of unsurpassed richness, and is one of the qualities that most inevitably endears him to the Englishman who has spent his life among them, and has, in consequence, acquired an almost native love for the wild and forbidding highland glens and their lawless denizens.

The Pathan has been dubbed cruel, treacherous, miserly, and, in fact, every epithet of an opprobrious nature has been showered on his devoted head at one time or another by men who were either incapable of seeing things from the Pathan point of view, and of making allowances for his shortcomings, or who were so hidebound by the humanity-mongering sentimentality which passes to-day for the hall-mark of a liberal mind that they shudderingly dismissed the Pathan from their thoughts (presumably with pious ejaculations) as an unreclaimable savage. And yet the same man, in all probability, would reserve a corner in his heart for Cesar Borgia, Louis XI., or King John, and even find an excuse for the atrocities of "Jack the Ripper" under the plea of *crime passionnel.* Here it may be as well to point out that the vast majority of murders committed on the North-

West Frontier, for which the unlucky perpetrator would in all probability receive a sentence of death from the horrified Pharisee, are actuated by jealousy; that the vast majority of raids into British territory are committed out of sheer hunger and desperation; and that nearly every attack on British officers or civilians has been carefully planned by bigoted and fanatical priests, who hold out to their ignorant and only too willing tools the prospect of paradise and salvation as the reward for the killing of a hated "unbeliever." As to his miserliness, it is the miserliness of him from whom has been taken even that which he had; and though the Pathan is undoubtedly acquisitive, yet he lacks the cunning to turn this trait to good account, and the moneylenders of Peshawar and Kabul, who grow fat on the duller wits of the Semitic Afghan and Pathan, are the Hindu "bannias," who are tolerated in the midst of the Mahommedan community on account of their business capacity, but who are, however, compelled to wear a distinctive headgear on account of their religion, consisting either of a red or yellow puggaree or a small skullcap. These are the colours of the Hindu religion, and for this reason the Mahommedan dons with the greatest reluctance the scarlet livery of the Sirkar.

But if the Pathan is unable to turn to advantage his miserly propensities, he knows full well how to dip his hook into the flesh-pots of the wealthy

Hindu bannias of Peshawar. Raids on Peshawar City itself in the old days were by no means an uncommon event, the last recorded being that which occurred early in 1908, when a band of from sixty to eighty Zakka Khel Afridis looted the Hindu quarter, always the first point to be made for, killing two policemen, wounding a score of men, and carrying off booty to the value of at least one lakh of rupees. It was this raid that heralded the despatch of an expedition against the Zakka Khel into the Bazar Valley. Since then the probability of successfully carrying out a raid on Peshawar has been materially reduced by the careful patrolling of the Peshawar border, and the immediate notification to all fortified posts, from Michni to Bara Fort, of the presence of any band of marauding tribes-people that may justly be suspected of being on the war-path. The opportunity of wrecking the Hindu quarter does, however, occur at certain intervals, when the coincidence of a Hindu and a Mahommedan festival causes racial feeling, and a riot ensues. Such a scene took place in March, 1910, when the Hindu festival of rejoicing (the "Holli") fell on the same day as the Mahommedan feast of mourning ("Barawafat"), when the mourners went about the streets, only to be pelted with bricks from the upper windows. The demise of one Mahommedan, who had been hit by one of the missiles, was the signal for a general rush to the Hindu quarter, which was incontinently stripped bare, the carpet-dealers losing practically the whole of their store of carpets, which had just arrived from Penjdeh. At such a time Peshawar is full of Musalmans from every part of Central Asia—Pathans, Ghilzais, Hazaras, Bokharans, Turcomans, Kabulis, and Heratis—and presents a curiously cosmopolitan aspect, so that it is truly said that when you have crossed the Indus you are no longer in India, but in Central Asia.

Situated as it is at the very mouth of the Khaibar Pass, and forming as it does the connecting link between Central Asia and Hindustan, it is natural that Peshawar should constitute the chief entrepôt for Central Asian trade, and therefore the political centre for frontier intrigue. Dera Ismail Khan, in the south of the province, fills the same position with regard to Waziristan and Southern Afghanistan, since it constitutes the point on which the pass-roads through the Suleiman Range converge. In a minor degree Kohat fulfils the same office for the Kurram and Tochi Valleys. But it is in Peshawar itself that the trained hand may keep its finger on the pulse of trans-border feeling, and in its bazaars that the first throb of unrest gives vague presage of trouble.

The city of Peshawar lies in a semicircular valley surrounded on all sides by mountains, low at first to the eastward, where the Kabul River and its muddy tributaries make their way to the Indus, but rising gradually as they sweep round to the north and to the south, until at length they culminate due west in the massive peak of Lakka, the highest point in the Tartarra or Khaibar Range, which stands sentinel over the most historic pass in the history of the world. From the Gorkatri, the palace of the Governor of the old Sikh province, situated in the centre of the town, a magnificent view can be obtained towards sunset of the encircling panorama, and on a clear day to the north-west may be descried the mountains of Bajaur, and in winter, perhaps, a glimpse of the snows on the summit of the far-away Lowari Pass, which for four solid months divides the little garrison of Chitral from the outside world. It was in this palace that the terrible Sikh Governor, General Avitábile, an Italian by birth, known to his subjects and to posterity as Abu Tabela, seated on a sumptuous divan, and attired in a flowing garment of red silk, dispensed a summary and somewhat primitive justice to the turbulent populace of Peshawar. It was his boast that he kept Peshawar in order by the simple expedient of hanging every week four of the most prominent citizens. Round the foot of this palace, and extending some way to the southward, lie the intricate and tortuous alleys, the mud hovels of the poor, the brick houses of the well-to-do, the bazaars of the coppersmiths and silversmiths, the leather-workers, the carpet-sellers, the silk-merchants, the tea-merchants, and a host of others, and in this labyrinth of filth and evil odours dwell 100,000 mysterious Orientals, here to-day and gone to-morrow, the places of those who leave for the passes always being filled by the constant stream of those that arrive. To stand at the western gate of the city and to watch the long files of camels as they dawdle past on their way to the "kafila-serai," gurgling and bellowing under their loads, is a liberal education in itself. Here a confused mass of long-haired, two-humped Bactrian camels, supporting enormous bales of carpets, block the way, and behind them comes a long string of the one-humped Arabian variety, with a contribution of old rags and malodorous asafœtida, to the general discomfiture of a mixed flock of "dumba," or fat-tailed Afghan sheep, long-eared goats, and small brown cattle. These are goaded on by lanky youths armed with stout sticks, and ancient white puggarees wound round their heads. Presently will come a buffalo moving stolidly forward under at least a ton of sugar-cane, while an Afghan, with pointed "culla," henna-dyed beard, a drab-coloured Poshtin coat embroidered with yellow silk, baggy white trousers caught in at the ankle, and curly-toed Peshauri shoon, all complete, jogs by on a mouse-coloured trotting donkey. All this vision of the teeming life of the frontier town is seen through a dense veil of dust, from out of which issues the raucous voice of invisible Jehus, bidding the unwary "Batchka! garhiwallah!" "Batchka! Apridiah!" (O Afridi), each in turn being apostrophized with unerring accuracy, according to the calling or the tribe to which his appearance indicates that he belongs;

while in the neighbouring caravanserai the long-suffering camel subsides like a collapsing suspension bridge, to the muttered exhortation of the camel-man, "Ush! Ush! be imana!" (Kneel! kneel! O dishonourable one!)

The Khaibar Pass itself is, of course, one of the principal places of pilgrimage for the traveller in India, attracting him from down-country wanderings with an almost hypnotic influence. I, too, was no stranger to these feelings, as in response to an invitation from Major Bickford, Commandant of the Khaibar Rifles, I hired a bazaar "tum-tum" (two-wheeled cart) and drove out through the long avenue of Peshawar Cantonment to spend a couple of days at Landi Kotal. Passing the lines of the Munsters and the 51st Sikhs, and the Guard House surrounded with barbed-wire entanglements as a precaution against rifle-stealers, we debouch upon the broad military road that leads straight as an arrow to the old Sikh fort of Jamrud. Parallel to us and on our left runs the single line of the Peshawar-Jamrud Railway, along which daily the "Flying Afridi" clanks and groans. Presently we reach Kacha Garhi, railway-station and fortified post, where the Kabul River Railway branches off northwards to its unknown terminus among the Mullagori Hills. Here I pick up my host, and we drive on to tiffin at Jamrud. On the way he points out to me the different landmarks in the surrounding country. To the north and north-west among those hills is the country of the Mohmands; to the west-south-west, behind a high ridge, the Bazar Valley; to the south lies Tirah and the Bara Valley, and a little farther to the eastward the low neck of the Kohat Pass. Among those low foothills on our left dwell two septs of the Kuki Khel Afridi, at deadly feud with one another. Their fortified villages may just be descried in a fold of the hills. This feud is carried on by means of artillery. Each village has an old muzzle-loading cannon, but between them they can only muster thirteen or fourteen cannon-balls, the remainder being presumably embedded in the mud-walls of the strongholds. These cannon-balls are solemnly fired backwards and forwards whenever the feud breaks out. The "game," of course, is to make a "corner" in cannon-balls, when terms may be dictated for the time being by the successful collector. But, like blackmail, the power which the possession of the cannon-balls gives is only efficacious as long as they remain unexpended. This never lasts for long, as the childish folk cannot long resist the intense pleasure of firing the cannon. From time to time we pass evil-looking scoundrels, who eye us with fierce and lowering brow, or perhaps their faces light up in answer to the cheery Pushtu salutation, "May you never be tired!" to which the invariable reply is, "May you never be poor!" The fact remains that the Afridi is poor—abjectly poor, though he is never tired.

The entrance to the Khaibar lies some two and

a half miles beyond Jamrud, and the change from the perfectly flat plain to the rocky, mountainous defile is very abrupt. Up and up leads the road in serpentine convolutions, doubling, twisting, writhing, until the Chargai Kotal is reached, with the Chargai Post perched on the top of an unscalable rock like a pinnacle of the temple. Here a gradual descent begins, and a little farther on the road up to the Chura Pass into the Bazar Valley is passed. It was close here that Sir Havelock Allan lost his life, shot by Afridis. And now the gorge begins to narrow, and the road sweeps down to Ali Masjid, situated at the narrowest and most forbidding portion of the pass. The ancient Sikh fortress, surmounted by the British fort, towers above, completely dominating the defile. Formerly the road lay along the bed of the streamlet, and one can well imagine the difficulties of its passage during the first Afghan War, and the awful reputation which it then gained. But since 1851 it runs along the northern scarp, though even now one can hardly repress a shudder at its dark and sombre aspect, so pregnant with disaster.

Between Ali Masjid and the first Zakka Khel village that announces the end of the pass, we had the misfortune to pass one of the longest kafilas that I saw, either here in subsequent visits to the Khaibar, or in the Kurram, or crossing the bed of the Indus at Dera Ismail Khan. There must have been fully 800 camels, peacefully plodding along on their way to Kabul, with what unknown merchandise for the Amir I could not imagine, unless it were cases of ·303 ammunition, and shell-fuses and such like contraband, carefully concealed among the bales of cotton and cloth, and in the square packing-cases. However, we managed eventually to overhaul the head of the caravan, with only a trifling damage, caused by a camel shying across the road with two enormous wooden packing-cases, with which he splintered our left mudguard. And now a few scattered fortified villages appear, belonging to Zakka Khel and Loargai Shinwari tribesmen, and the valley widens out as Landi Kotal is reached, twenty-seven miles from Peshawar.

A short distance from Landi Kotal is a hill, which, from the commanding view that can be obtained from its summit of the "promised land," Afghanistan, has been dubbed "Pisgah." This we ascended late in the afternoon, and gazed out over the confusion of mountain-tops to the Jellalabad Plain, where the last rays of the setting sun were sparkling on the far-away water of the Kabul River, somewhere in the neighbourhood of Dakka Fort—at least, so it seemed to me, although my eyes may have deceived me. Northward, in the faint distance, lay the massive range of the Hindu Kush, and in between the cone-like peaks of Kafiristan. To the south-west, through a vista in the hills above Landi Khana, a single white peak of the Sofed Koh gleamed like alabaster against the granite coldness of the nearer range—perhaps the peak of Sikaram above Parachinar in Kurram, full 15,000 feet high.

Up here it was quite chilly, the month being December, and we returned to the warm fire in the mess-room of the Khaibar Rifles in the fort, after paying a visit to the men's quarters and watching them prepare their evening meal of chupatties, curried dal, and rice. Chupatties are merely unleavened pancakes made of flour, water, and ghee (clarified butter), baked on an iron girdle. Dal is a kind of lentil. We also entered the hospital in the fort, in which at the time there were no sepoys. There were, however, a few sick tribesmen from the surrounding villages, suffering from bronchitis, cataract, and other diseases, and a Laghman Afghan, who had sustained a severe wound in some trans-border affray. He was being nursed by his own father, who had brought him in. The surest way to the heart of an Afghan or a Pathan is the ability to heal him, and this certainly accounts for the personal immunity with which the famous "daktar-sahib" of Bannu, the Rev. Mr. Pennell, can move about in independent tribal territory, an "unbeliever" in a Muslim country, and for the respect in which he is held by the usually so fanatical mullas.

On the following day, in company with Major Bickford and Captain Galbraith, 55th Coke's Rifles, P.F.F., I walked down to the Afghan frontier at Torkham, past the enormous mud-walled kafila-serai just outside Landi Kotal, and past the block-house at Michni Kandao, which was attacked by an Afghan "lashkar" during the Mohmand rising of 1908. Beyond this is the first Afghan post of Paindi Kakh. The boundary here has never been properly delimited, and the Afghans in consequence lay claim to the water-supply at Landi Khana, between Tor Kham and Michni Kandao, with the object of gaining control over the stream which rises here and drains into the Kabul River below Dakka Fort. The question of water-supply is always a very important one in a country where practically every crop depends on irrigation.

The inhabitants of the villages round Landi Kotal live chiefly by carrying firewood into Peshawar, and this also is the principal occupation of the poorer cave-dwelling Afridis, whose caves we had passed on our way up the Khaibar. To me it is a mystery where the wood comes from, as I never saw a tree of any kind, or even a shrub capable of producing firewood, except the sorry scrub that occasionally crops up in barren and unexpected places. As a second string to his bow, when firewood fails, the resourceful Afridi can always support life by raiding.

To the north of Landi Kotal lies the little-known territory of the Shilmanis and Mullagoris, dwelling on the right bank of the Kabul River. These two tribes inhabit the natural cul-de-sac formed by the great northerly bend that the Kabul River takes below Dakka Fort. Through this country runs the Mullagori Road and the almost legendary Kabul River Railway, as alternative strategic routes from Peshawar. From the walls of Landi Kotal one may see the road stretching away to the north-east as far as the kandao which forms the southern barrier of the Kam Shilman Valley. What lies beyond is veiled in mystery. Torkamr—the point to which the Kabul River Railway was sanctioned by Parliament—is a mere geographical expression as far as the outside world is concerned. The difficulty of railway construction in the narrow gorge of the Kabul River may be apprehended from the heated discussions that took place over the selection of the route. We know that the railway never reached Torkamr, although the "flying Afridi" runs as far as Warsak,* the last station in the Peshawar plain.

The reasons for the construction of the Kabul River Railway are to be found in the inadequacy of the Khaibar roads for the rapid despatch of a large army into Afghanistan, and for provisioning it when there. Supposing we ever had occasion to send an army into Afghanistan, this one avenue is easily interrupted, flanked as it is on both sides by presumably hostile Afridi tribes. In any case this road would never be sufficient for supplying a body of, say, from 60,000 to 100,000 men, and so it was thought advisable to have alternative routes. In

* This Warsak must not be confused with the Warsak in the Loe Shilman Valley.

pursuance of this line of policy the Mullagori Road was constructed, and the Loe Shilman or Kabul River Railway sanctioned as far as Torkamr. In a later chapter we shall see what trouble arose out of its construction. Beyond Torkamr a discussion arose as to the best route to be followed to the Afghan frontier. Lord Kitchener, then Commander-in-Chief, advocated a direct route westward up the Loe Shilman Valley, thence through a tunnel to the west of Warsak to the village of Smatsai, below Dakka Fort. But, principally on account of the expense that the construction of this tunnel would have entailed, it was eventually decided to follow the course of the Kabul River upstream along the big northerly bend past Palosi, a route which presented fewer engineering difficulties. Ultimately further construction was postponed. It is to be hoped that this decision was dictated by consideration of real policy, and not by the wave of economy which from time to time seems to sweep over the India Office, like a plague of locusts, blighting every progressive or expedient measure it may happen to encounter.

Though by no means so frequented by former invaders of India as the Khaibar Pass, this route was undoubtedly known to the ancients, and would, indeed, be a more rational route to follow than the narrow and tortuous Khaibar, inhabited by the warlike Aparytæ (Afridi), as Herodotus calls them. Though a portion of Alexander's troops made the passage of the Khaibar, the majority are supposed to have gone by the more northerly route. The old camel-road of the Buddhist pilgrims exists also, which was, and, I believe, still is, used on occasion by the Amir's "dak-runners" as an alternative to the Khaibar.

CHAPTER II

THE ZAKKA KHEL AND MOHMAND EXPEDITIONS

"'Tis War, red War, I'll give you then,
War till my sinews fail;
For a wrong you have done to a Chief of Men,
And a Thief of the Zakka Kheyl."

KIPLING: *Lament of the Border Cattle Thief.*

SINCE the final quelling of the revolt of 1897 in Tirah, the Afridi border had remained comparatively peaceful, but for the spasmodic raiding of various bands of outlaws, until in 1904 it again began to respond to the secret machinations of the fanatical Anglophobe party in Kabul. In that year large numbers of Afridis visited the Afghan metropolis, being well received by the Amir, and sent away with presents of money, after having purchased considerable quantities of arms and ammunition. Friendly relations with Kabul were still further cemented with the assistance of one Khawwas Khan, an ex-malik of the Zakka Khel and a former citizen of Peshawar, through whose instrumentality the Afridi clans were enabled more and more to count on the support of a powerful faction among the counsellors of the Amir. In fact, to such a

SKETCH MAP OF
THE DISTRICTS OF
PESHAWAR, KOHAT, BANNU
AND
DERA ISMAIL KHAN.

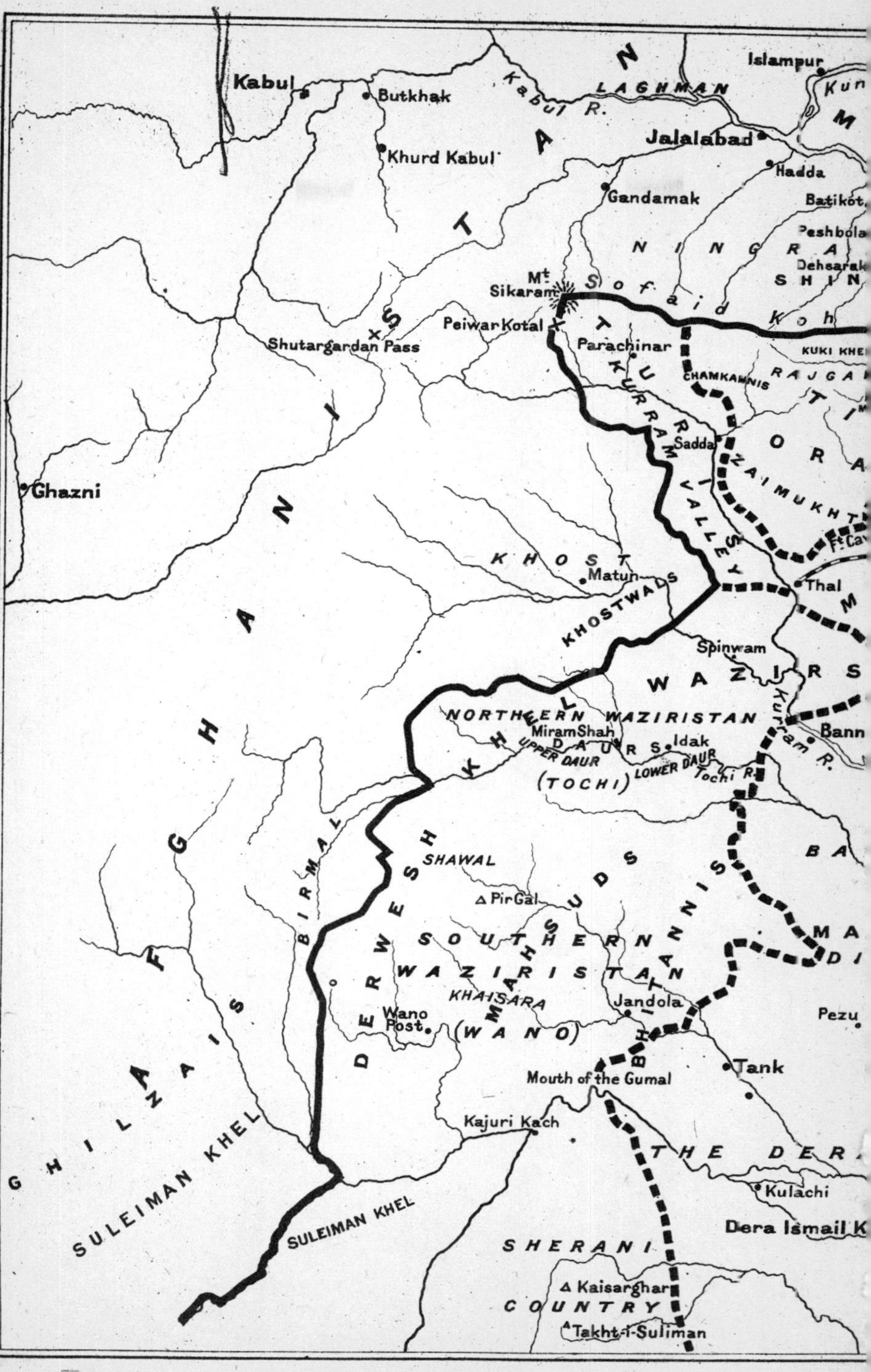

AFGHANISTAN
Kabul
Butkhak
Kabul R.
LAGHMAN
Islampur
Kun
Jalalabad
Hadda
Khurd Kabul
Gandamak
Batikot
Peshbola
NINGRAHAR
Dehsarak
SHIN
Mt. Sikaram
Sofaid Koh
Peiwar Kotal
Shutargardan Pass
Parachinar
KUKI KHEL
CHAMKANNIS
RAJGAL
KURRAM VALLEY
TURIS
Sadda
ZAIMUKHTS
ORAKZAI
Ft. Cav
Thal
Ghazni
KHOST
Matun
KHOSTWALS
Spinwam
WAZIRS
NORTHERN WAZIRISTAN
Miram Shah
DAURS
Idak
UPPER DAUR
LOWER DAUR
(TOCHI)
Tochi R.
Kurram R.
Bann
KHEL
BIRMAL
DERWESH
SHAWAL
Pir Gal
MAHSUDS
SOUTHERN WAZIRISTAN
KHAISARA
Wano Post
(WANO)
Jandola
BHITANNIS
Pezu
Tank
Mouth of the Gumal
Kajuri Kach
THE DERA
Kulachi
Dera Ismail K
GHILZAIS
SULEIMAN KHEL
SULEIMAN KHEL
SHERANI COUNTRY
Kaisarghar
Takht-i-Suliman

degree did this man gain an ascendancy over the mind of the Amir that the latter was wholly unable, when the time came, to prevent the insurrection which the Afridis were emboldened to make, relying on the support which his actions had given good cause for anticipating. Through Khawwas Khan and his myrmidons it was that the Afridis and the Mohmands, and even the Shinwaris, were gradually worked up to the belief that the time had come when the English should be driven back over the Indus by a general uprising of the independent tribes, in which Afghan lashkars would play no inconspicuous part. All through the year 1904 raids were frequent, and the Afridi allowances were stopped for a time. But though this had a salutary effect on the majority of the clans, the Zakka Khel continued to be the ringleaders in the raiding, and when the allowances were once more renewed, the Zakka Khel were excluded from the number. The defiant and uncompromising attitude of the Zakka Khel was no doubt due to the constant assurances of Khawwas Khan that they had nothing to fear, as well as to the fact that the Zakka Khel are the poorest and most "jungly" of all the Afridi clans, and have come least into contact with British rule. Situated as they are at the farthest point of Tirah from British territory, and the nearest to Afghanistan, they would be more susceptible to Afghan influences, and less likely to appreciate the probable consequences of their temerity. Their territory would also afford to the outlaws the surest sanctuary, and having already forfeited their allowances, they would as soon be hung for a sheep as for a lamb. Among the chief of the outlaws may be mentioned Dadai, Usman, and Multan, all of whom were notorious for the number of their crimes and the daring with which they were carried out. These three went constantly to Kabul, where they listened eagerly to the rash and malignant scheming of Khawwas Khan, returning to Tirah only to confirm the Zakka Khel more surely in their folly. The Shinwari mullas were also untiring in their efforts to bring about a crisis in Tirah and among the Mohmands, who were also at this time showing signs of disaffection on account of the construction of the Loe Shilman or Kabul River Railway, which they regarded as a prelude to the taking over of their country. In this connection, Alam Gul, the "Sufi Sahib" of Batikot, was the most indefatigable, dividing his attention equally between Tirah and the Mohmands. This gentleman, like the "Gud Mulla" (or Lame Mulla) of Inzari, was a disciple of the well-known Hadda Mulla, a native of the Jellalabad district, who in 1897, with a following of Afghans, had raided Shankargarh on the Mohmand border, and attacked the fort of Shabkadr. His anti-British propaganda had begun some years before, when in 1902 a new allowance had been granted to the Musa Khel Baezai Mohmands, which afforded him an excellent opportunity of denouncing the recipients as "kafirs," with the result that the Musa Kheī and other Mohmand clans did not come in to receive their due.

Another principal cause for the suspicion and mistrust with which we were regarded at this time by the Mohmands was the proposed Mohmand Boundary Commission, which was intended to do away with the facility with which Afghan Mohmands could raid into what, strictly speaking, had been laid down as British territory by the Durand Agreement. Major (now Sir George) Roos-Keppel was deputed as the British Representative, and it was arranged that he should meet the Afghan Commissioners at the Nawa Kotal in Mohmand territory on February 1, 1903, and mark out the boundary, as far as the crest of the Sofaid Koh at the Peiwar Kotal in the Kurram, to the south of the Khaibar. But owing to the obstructive measures of the Amir, the Boundary Commission never started. If it had, it is quite possible that the British members of it would never have returned. During the construction of the Loe Shilman Railway the Tarakzai and Halimzai Mohmands, as well as the Mullagoris on the southern bank, who had undertaken to protect the line from attack, were repeatedly subjected to annoyances from the Afghan Mohmands. The Sarhang of Dakka especially showed a particular desire to pick a quarrel at any price and on any pretext, with the object of impeding the progress of the work. A dispute arose as to the ownership of logs and driftwood which the inhabitants of Smatsai, a small village on the right bank of the Kabul River a little below Dakka, had been accustomed to collect for fuel. The Sarhang attacked the village, and, on a remonstrance from the British Government, claimed Smatsai as lying in Afghan territory. Whatever the justice of this claim, and it appears that the words of the Durand Agreement admit of a considerable elasticity of interpretation, we, at any rate, were perfectly justified in not recognizing the claim, seeing that it was through the obstructionist attitude of the Amir that the boundary had remained undemarcated. Thus in 1905 for the second time the question of demarcation was raised, only to come again to the same infructuous end. Meanwhile attacks on the Kabul River Railway, under the instigation of Sahib Haq, Akhundzada, son of the Mulla Khalil, occurred as before, and numerous raids were committed by such notorious outlaws as Mahazil, Khoda Khel Baezai, and Hakim Khan,* on the unprotected villages of the Mohmand border. The reinforcement of the frontier posts at this point led, however, to a temporary cessation of these annoyances.

During 1907 the Zakka Khel, in spite of the genuine efforts of the maliks of the remaining Afridi clans to restrain them, adopted a yet more

* The notorious outlaw Hakim Khan, with a following of twenty-nine, was taken near the village of Char Sadda on February 28, 1911. Hakim and twenty of his accomplices were killed, and the rest were captured and suffered death by hanging.

defiant attitude towards the British Government, and an Afridi jirga met at Landi Kotal in that year to deliberate on what steps should be taken to abate the nuisance. During this meeting and while the Afridi maliks were urging on the Government the advisability of occupying the Bazar Valley, a Zakka Khel jirga made its appearance, professing itself willing to come to terms. Not content with offering an unconditional surrender, the Zakka Khel in their turn made such preposterous and absurd demands, conditions, and stipulations, that the insincerity of their professions was made only too apparent, and they were immediately dismissed.

All this time the progress of the unrest was being watched with jealous care in Kabul, and secret agents continued to send in their quota of information to the leaders of the Anglophobe party. It is probable that at this time the Amir began to realize the nature of the whirlwind that was about to be reaped from the insignificant wind that had been sown by the presence of Khawwas Khan in Kabul.* Early in 1907 the Sufi Sahib, accompanied by Abdul Karim, a Shinwari of Deh Sarak, was preaching a "jehad" in Tirah, while Lala Pir, a secret agent from Kabul, was engaged in stirring up the tribes in Khost and Waziristan, and holding communication with the Mulla Powindah and the Hamzullah

* The *Pioneer* had repeatedly urged on the Government of India the advisability of obtaining the dismissal of Khawwas Khan from Kabul.

Mulla, with the intent to incite the Wazirs and Mahsuds to revolt. Unsuccessful in Waziristan, he turned his attention to Khost, where, on the outbreak of hostilities, he raised a lashkar, which was to have co-operated with a Ghilzai lashkar from the Ghazni district in an attack on the Kurram Valley. Among the Mohmands and Ningraharis the "Hazrat Sahib" of Chaharbagh, Fidai Masun Jan, succeeded, with the help of the Sufi Sahib and the Gud Mulla, in raising a lashkar, principally composed of Afghan Mohmands and Shinwaris.

The Afridi maliks having proved themselves utterly incapable of exercising any influence over the Zakka Khel, the Government, after clutching at every straw that seemed to hold out a possibility of a settlement, suddenly sanctioned an expedition, as the result of a determined raid on Peshawar City undertaken by Multan and other outlaws on the night of January 28, 1908. This raid occurred in spite of the fact that the whole of the Jamrud, Bara, and Kohat Pass roads were being patrolled at the time. Three constables were wounded, two of whom died, and the raiding-party escaped over the city wall before any reinforcements could be brought up.

As soon as the intelligence was received by the Zakka Khels that punitive operations had been sanctioned against them, they began moving their families and flocks and herds through the passes into Ningrahar, whither also the outlaws Multan,

Dadai, and Usman also repaired, returning, however, to take part in the fighting. The Chief Commissioner of the North-West Frontier Province, Colonel Deane, summoned the Afridi maliks to a jirgà in Peshawar, where he made it plain to them that the object of the expedition was merely to punish the Zakka Khel, and that no annexation of territory was in any way contemplated. This very timely declaration of our intentions had the very beneficial effect of securing to us the co-operation of the Afridi maliks throughout the campaign, in spite of the untiring efforts of Mulla Saiyid Akbar, Aka Khel, one of the ringleaders in 1897, to raise them. They were, in fact, induced to maintain a blockade of the passes from the Bazar Valley into Tirah, so that the passes into Afghanistan were the only avenues of supply for the leaguered Zakka Khel. It was proposed to take up two brigades into Bazar, and to hold one brigade in readiness at Nowshera. Major-General Sir James Willcocks was given full military and political control of the expedition, and Lieutenant-Colonel Roos-Keppel acted as Political Officer. The value to the Zakka Khel of one, at least, of the passes into Ningrahar was largely discounted by the rapidity with which this latter officer led a flying column into Bazar by way of the Bazar Pass, which opens out of the Khaibar a little short of Ali Masjid. By sending part of his baggage animals back from Ali Masjid to Jamrud, the Zakka Khel were led to believe that no entry was intended by way of the Bazar Pass;

consequently the column was enabled to make the passage unopposed, and thus get between the Zakka Khel and their bolt-holes into Afghanistan, at the same time gaining possession of the village of China, commanding these exits. The second brigade entered the valley by the Chura Pass through Malikdin Khel country, and advanced to Walai, while the first brigade occupied Chura.

Mountain warfare, as carried on on the North-West Frontier, does not lend itself to impassioned descriptions of bloody fields of battle, of cavalry charges and heroic actions done in the limelight before the astounded gaze of two armies. The Afridi does not rush down into the open to certain death, but retires gracefully before a stronger force sent against him, skulking along the sky-line, and ready to take advantage of the smallest mistake on the part of his opponents, or to cut off any straggler. He has been described as the finest natural skirmisher in the world. It is when the retirement of the British troops begins that he is at his best, and then it is that those deeds of heroism are committed by our British and Indian troops alike, when there is none to mark how those battery mules were got safely across that open nulla-bed, swept as it was, by a hail of bullets, or how So-and-so held on to an almost isolated position, at the risk of being cut off, for three minutes more than was necessary, in order to enable a wounded comrade or two to get a good start down the hill. At night, too, worn out and dog-tired by the constant hill-climbing, the soldier must cook and eat his food in the dark, as no lights are allowed, for fear of attracting the fire of the snipers. Then he must dig himself into a narrow trench in the ground, and hope for sleep, while from the hills around an incessant firing is kept up till daylight. Those who by repeated experience of this kind of warfare may be considered competent judges declare that nothing is more nerve-racking or more demoralizing to troops than to have to undergo night after night this constant sniping, coupled with the apprehension of a night attack at any moment. The first indication of a night attack is like the rustling of the wind through autumn leaves, as the "chaplis" of the silent-footed foe slither over the rocky ground; then follows the confused, half-audible jingle of accoutrements, steel upon steel, and jangling neck ornaments, and the final rush and the blood-curdling pandemonium that is let loose as the wave of savagery breaks on the bristling perimeter of the camp. Occasionally one of those little incidents occurs which serve to relieve the tension and raise a smile all round, even though it be but a false alarm in the middle of the night, caused by an inconsiderate sepoy falling asleep with his shoulder against the firing-button of a machine-gun.

At the beginning of the operations the Amir had issued a declaration to his subjects forbidding them to join in the hostilities, but in spite of this and of his presence so close to the scene as Jellalabad, large numbers of Sangu Khel Shinwaris, Afghan

Mohmands and Ningraharis of every description, entered the Bazar Valley by the Tsatsobi Pass, where they openly sold ammunition to the rebels, aided them in fighting, and proved particularly obnoxious by militating in every possible manner against the resumption of peaceful relations with the Zakka Khel. With fanatical zeal, they exhorted them not to conclude peace with us at any price, with the consequence that negotiations were conducted with the greatest difficulty, and our occupation of the valley was much longer than it need have been. At their instigation, too, the Zakka Khel sent messages to the Mohmands urging them to rise, and the Hazrat Sahib and the Sufi Sahib did everything that could be done to bring about a combined insurrection. But at length the Zakka Khel, having exhausted ammunition, supplies, and means alike, and having seen their fortified villages disappear skywards in a cloud of dust, were brought to their knees, and terms were at length agreed to through the mediation of the Afridi jirga. These latter undertook to punish the outlaws, to guarantee each a section of the Zakka Khel, and to deposit so many rifles until the Political Officer should consider that the Zakka Khel had sufficiently expiated their folly. The outlaw Dadai died of the wounds he had sustained, cursing Khawwas Khan and his own folly in bringing desolation on his clan.

The difficulties attending the satisfactory termination of the Zakka Khel rising were enhanced by the necessity of keeping a watchful eye simultaneously on other parts of the frontier. Hardly a month elapsed before it again became necessary to send a punitive force into independent territory—this time against the Mohmands. All through February and the first fortnight in April, raiding had been increasing on the Abazai border, and the Shinwari lashkar that had collected in Ningrahar at the close of the Zakka Khel Expedition crossed the Kabul River at Lalpura and went off to throw in their lot with the Mohmands. The constant influx from the Afghan side led to reinforcements being early sent to the forts of Michni and Shankargarh. After telegraphic communications had been twice interrupted, villages raided, and posts fired on, it was at length decided to mobilize a second expedition under the command of General Willcocks. Brigadier-General Anderson, Major-General Barrett, and Major-General Ramsay, had command of Brigades, the Third Brigade being held in reserve. On April 24 two columns attacked the enemy's position west of Shankargarh, and the enemy were driven back with heavy loss. This defeat greatly discouraged the mullas, who were trying to raise Dir and Swat. At the same time every effort made to gain the co-operation of the Zakka Khel and the Loargai Shinwaris proved unsuccessful, and many mullas retired in consequence into Afghanistan. The Mohmands' supplies were now running short, and many combatants availed themselves of the dead or wounded among their relations to accompany them back into Ningrahar, whence they were careful not to return. The Hazrat Sahib, however, doggedly remained in Mohmand country, though with a greatly reduced following, gradually retiring into the more remote valleys of that district. In Tirah the maliks had been successful in counteracting the efforts of Mullah Saiyid Akbar to raise the Afridis, in spite of the latter's invitation to the Sufi Sahib to join him in the Lower Bara Valley, whilst in the Bazar Valley what Zakka Khels yet remained—the majority having gone up into Maidan for the summer—intimated that they would oppose the Sufi's lashkar, if necessary, with force. The Mohmand trouble appeared to be dying a natural death, and the Government of India had already intimated to General Willcocks that no advance should be made into Mohmand country if it could possibly be avoided, when a diversion of a dangerous nature suddenly arose in the Khaibar. On April 29 the Mian Sahib of Tsappar arrived at Peshbolak in Ningrahar with a Khugiani lashkar some 6,000 strong. A junction with the force already assembled under the Sufi Sahib and other mullas brought the total of the combined lashkars up to nearly 20,000.

This formidable gathering, which was composed entirely of Afghans, moved up to Landi Khana, part of it, under the Sufi Sahib, entering Bazar. The fortified post of Michni Kandao, just below Landi Kotal, was attacked on the nights of May 2 and 3, and General Willcocks moved up to Landi Kotal with reinforcements, with which on the following day he drove the Sufi's lashkar across the Afghan boundary.

As a result of this sudden and unexpected reverse to the Afghan supporters of the Mohmands, the Hazrat Sahib's following suffered a further decrease in numbers, and the voice of the Amir, which had been raised in half-audible protestations to which nobody paid any attention, now thundered forth in an authoritative recall of all subjects of His Majesty from independent territory. But by this time no such command was needed to insure the rapid exodus of Afghans from the Mohmand borders, though, no doubt, the Amir congratulated himself on his (somewhat tardy) loyalty to his treaty engagements with the English.

Up till this time only two of the Mohmand clans—namely, the Halimzai and the Pandiali Mohmands—had ventured to come in. The remainder had been deterred from following this example, probably by the fear that the Government contemplated an annexation of Mohmand territory.* These two clans undertook to induce the remaining sections to come in, and May 9 was fixed as the date by which their submission should take place. With the exception of the Musa Khel section of the Baezai, the Baezai and Khwaezai

* The Halimzai and Tarakzai Mohmands, as well as the Shilmanis and Mullagoris who live on the southern bank of the Kabul River, remained loyal to the Government throughout the campaign.

are considered as Afghan subjects. The remaining Mohmand clans consisted of the Utmanzai, Dawezai, Isa Khel, Burhan Khel, and the Musâ Khel Baezai. Nothing having occurred by May 9, the First and Second Brigades advanced into Mohmand territory. On May 15 the column arrived at the Kharappa and Nahaki Passes, in the Gundab Valley, without opposition. The enemy were, however, found in considerable force in the Khapak Pass, having been joined by Baezai and Khwaezai Afghan Mohmands. The efforts of the First Brigade were directed against the Kandahari Sufis, while the Second Brigade ascended the valley of the Bohai Dag towards Kargha and Mulla Killai, in Utman Khel territory. By May 27 all the clans, with the exception of the Musa Khel Baezai, had tendered their submission, and, the latter having been punished on the following day, the troops began to evacuate Mohmand territory, which was effected by June 1.

CHAPTER III

THE POLICY OF THE AMIR

FOR close on half a century the nightmare of a Russian invasion of India through the passes of the Hindu Kush, or by way of Herat and the Parapomisus, has held the mind of the British public, clogging our foreign policy and forcing the hand of our diplomacy. In spite of the fact that since 1873 British statesmen have from time to time attempted to reassure the nation on this point, in no field of politics have alarmists and scaremongers obtained such a ready hearing as in this one of the Russian advance in Central Asia.

It is not necessary at this distance of time, and in view of our present relations with Russia, to rake up old scores, too highly coloured for the most part with the hues of national animus, but it may not be irrelevant to the subject to recall a few of the less hasty views of those British statesmen who, in the midst of the almost universal panic, still kept their heads.

In 1873 the Tsar had already intimated to the British Government, through Prince Gortchakoff, that he considered Afghanistan as lying altogether outside the Russian sphere of influence, an assurance which Lord Granville saw no reason for not accepting. But in 1868 the capture of Samarkand had caused such an ebullition of feeling in England that Lord Clarendon felt constrained to inform Baron Brunnow that "although Her Majesty's Government feel neither suspicion nor alarm at these movements, yet something must be done to allay the uneasiness of the British and Indian public." A scheme was then discussed for the establishment of a neutral zone in Central Asia, resembling somewhat the present so-called neutral zone in Persia: a scheme which was afterwards abandoned when the object for which it had been broached—namely, the pacification of the English public—had been for the time being attained.*

When in 1878, after the Treaty of San Stefano, we sent Indian troops to the Mediterranean, Skobeleff's plan, in the event of war breaking out between England and Russia, and provided he could gain the support of Shere Ali, was to make an invasion of India through the passes of the Hindu Kush. But it may be reasonably doubted that he would ever have contemplated such a step had he not fully believed that the whole of India was ready, at the mere approach of the Russians, to break out into a blaze of insurrection resembling the Mutiny of 1857.

It is a noticeable fact that, with one exception,

* Wheeler's "Life of Abdurrahman," practically the only really impartial review of the Russian question.

friction between Russia and England in Central Asia had always been preceded by strained relations between the two countries in Europe. This one exception was the "Penjdeh Incident" of 1885, when Gladstone's Parliament voted £11,000,000 for war preparations. The incident might easily have been avoided had we shown a little more firmness at the outset, and it is not at all clear that the Russians were prepared to back their views by resorting to extreme measures. Sir West Ridgeway, who succeeded Sir Peter Lumsden in command of the Boundary Commission, was of opinion that the Russians could not possibly have risked a war in view of the disturbed condition of the Mahommedan population under Russian rule at that time.*

To look for a moment at the Russian side of the question, a fact too often overlooked by the partisan historians of this period is that from 1868-1873 we, too, had caused the Russians considerable anxiety by our attempts, culminating in the Forsyth Mission, to establish commercial relations with Yakoub Beg of Kashgar. We had, in fact, ourselves been setting the example in what we afterwards complained so much of in Russia.

But to return to the question of the Russian invasion. Sir Donald Wallace, in his book "Russia," sums up the whole question in one pithy sentence:

* Wheeler's "Life of Abdurrahman," practically the only really impartial review of the Russian question.

"What *had* been seriously entertained, not only in the official world, but by the (Russian) Government itself, is the idea, strongly advocated by General Skobeleff, that Russia should as quickly as possible get within striking distance of our Indian possessions, so that she may always be able to bring strong diplomatic pressure to bear on the British Government, and, in the event of a conflict, immobilize a large part of the British army."

This places the whole matter in a much more reasonable and probable light, and is a strong argument against the notion that Russia ever harboured designs *per se* for the invasion of India.

Lastly, Lord Hardinge of Penshurst, at a banquet given for him on the eve of his departure for India by the county of Kent, said in reference to this question: "I have grave doubts as to whether such projects were ever seriously contemplated in those days by the Russians."

The elimination of the Russian question for the present from the sphere of practical politics on the North-West Frontier of India, if it cannot be said to have simplified the problems with which we are called upon to deal, at any rate must have the effect of modifying our policy in many of its hitherto most important aspects.

The situation now resolves itself into the three-cornered problem of—

1. Our relations with the Amir.
2. Our relations with the independent tribes.
3. Tribal relations with the Amir.

For the first time since the Vienna Congress of 1815, England is found acting in harmony with Russia, and the immediate consequence of this is that Afghanistan finds herself completely isolated. Hitherto the Amir's chief weapon has been his power to hold the balance between the two countries, and to play off England against Russia. He can now no longer count on the moral support of Russia in any situation where the interests of Great Britain and Afghanistan clash. We are, of course, still bound by our defensive treaty of alliance in the event of a foreign invasion of Afghanistan; and Russia, within the last two years or so, has renewed her assurances to us that she considers Afghanistan as lying altogether outside the sphere in which she may be called upon to act. At the same time, as long as the Amir observes the treaty negotiated in Kabul in 1905 by Sir Louis Dane, in which Habibullah undertook to be bound by the engagements that his father made with the Government of India, we are also bound to fulfil our side of the bargain, and to respect the independence of Afghanistan as a kingdom. By one of the Articles of the Durand Agreement of 1893 the Amir undertook not to exercise any interference in the independent territories on our side of the Durand line; but so often have risings among the border tribes been directly traceable to Afghan machinations as to lay Habibullah open to the charge of having violated, by commission or omission, this clause of his agreement.

What conceivable circumstances can be urged in defence of the following, or in what way can Habibullah seek to justify them? The reception of tribal jirgas in Kabul, either by the Amir or by Nasrullah, and their dismissal with gifts of money and arms; the presence of the proscribed ex-malik, Khawwas Khan, in Kabul, who attained such influence in the Amir's councils as ultimately to bring about a rising in the Bazar Valley; the open sale of rifles and ammunition to the Zakka Khel during the ensuing expedition, in direct defiance of the Amir's orders, and in spite of his presence not twenty miles away, at Jellalabad; finally, that a nest of outlaws should be permitted to exist in Khost, upon our very borders, and that no measures should be taken to put a stop to their depredations, until the capture of a native officer of a frontier militia rendered unpleasant complications with the Government of India an immediate possibility.

Whether personally guilty or not guilty, it is with Habibullah, as ruler of Afghanistan, that responsibility must ultimately rest. That such things should be possible calls for measures that shall arrest, once and for all, this gradual stultification of the Durand Agreement. The time has, in fact, come when we should intimate to him in no equivocal manner that relations of any political nature, either directly or indirectly, cannot longer be tolerated in independent territory. For, in the absence of the fanatical emissaries of the Kabul

Anglophobe party, the maliks have shown themselves, on the whole, capable of looking after the tribes under their charge, and inclined to discourage close relations with Afghanistan.

The exact attitude of the Amir towards us is a subject on which considerable difference of opinion exists. Whilst full of protestations of good-will towards us, he is sometimes so backward in giving practical effect to them as to furnish legitimate cause for doubting his sincerity. No doubt he is saddled with a difficult task in properly fulfilling his treaty obligations, and at the same time preserving his character among the Afghans as an uncompromising upholder of Afghan integrity and independence. To this and to the fact that his brother, Nasrullah Khan, has ever evinced the most thoroughgoing antagonism to everything British, may be attributed his waning popularity. It may even be doubted whether his popularity at any time since his visit to Hindustan would have been sufficient to keep him upon the throne but for the loyalty of his brother, who exercises by far the greater influence of the two, and who would probably be received with the greatest acclamation by the people did he choose to proclaim himself. However, at his accession he at least had the foresight to win over the soldiery by the simple expedient of increasing its pay, an operation which he has repeated at intervals since, although compelled to disband the inferior portion of his troops in order to defray the increasing cost of upkeep. But since

Nasrullah is Commander-in-Chief, it seems improbable that Habibullah could count on the undivided loyalty, except against an external foe, of any but the Kabul garrison.

Habibullah has been described as too easy-going to attempt any curtailment of Nasrullah's influence, relying, no doubt, on the Government of India to see him through any family crisis; and though Nasrullah has a great affection for his brother, he is said to have been much displeased at the nomination of Inayatullah, the Amir's son, as successor to the throne. It is also rumoured that Nasrullah is physically afraid of the Amir, and that when circumstances of a sufficiently peremptory nature have decided the latter on a definite course, the remonstrances of the Commander-in-Chief are swept away as chaff before the storm.

As Commander-in-Chief of the army, and at the same time spiritual head of the community and chief prop of the State, Nasrullah is to all outward appearances a dictator. Like the warrior-bishop of the Middle Ages, he is keenly alive to the advantages of combining the spiritual with the temporal power, and it is to the acquisition of supreme spiritual power that all his stealthy energies have been directed. Well he knows that in a country like Afghanistan, where the fanatical zeal and warlike propensities of the population are shrewdly turned to account by the mullas, whose only principles are subordinated to motives of political expediency and to the preservation of their own influence, the acquisition of such power is the passport to ultimate supremacy. In this he has been aided by circumstances. According to Musalman law anyone who, having prayed after the "chief imam" or preacher in the mosque, afterwards acts contrary to his commands, is counted an infidel, and ceases to belong to the company of the faithful. Most Afghans at one time or another have prayed after Nasrullah in his capacity of chief imam in the large open-air Masjid-i-pul-i-Pukhtu in Kabul, a mosque capable of accommodating several thousand people. Among these are sure to have been many tribespeople from our side the border, and hence it is not too much to say that it is only necessary for Nasrullah to despatch a body of mullas to preach a holy war against the British to cause in response a movement of unrest along the whole length of the frontier.

The first instinct of an Oriental monarch on ascending the throne is to get rid of all superfluous members of his family who may be suspected of any leanings towards the purple. This is effected by banishment or by harsher methods. At his death in 1823 Timur Shah left twenty-three sons, all of whom, during the disputed succession which followed, gradually disappeared, until only Shah Shujah and Dost Mahommed were left. Forty years later, on the death of the Dost, there was another disputed succession, many of the actors in which are still living in exile in either Russia or British India. On his accession Habibullah was spared the inconvenience of asserting his right to the throne, owing to the thoroughness with which his father, the lamented Abdurrahman, had previously cleared the country of all possible claimants. Yakoub Khan and Ayoub Khan, the sons of Shere Ali, who fled from Afghanistan in 1879, are now at Lahore, and, though both are over sixty years of age, probably still have some adherents among the Afghan Mohmands, their mother having been a lady of that tribe, a sister of Sa'adat Khan of Lalpura. A still more ancient link with the past survives in the person of Is'hak Khan, now over seventy years of age, if, indeed, he still lives, and an exile in Samarkand, Habibullah's birthplace. In fact, with the exception of his brother Nasrullah and of his half-brother, Mohammed Umar, a grandson of Shere Ali, a quarrelsome and irascible youth from all accounts, there has been no one who could show any pretence to the throne. For some years Bibi Halima, the mother of Mohammed Umar, was the cause of considerable friction at Kabul, but since Mohammed Umar (who never participated in the ambitious schemes his mother entertained for his future) slew the Amir's Master of Horse in a fit of passion, and on another occasion wounded Nasrullah in a quarrel, he has been allowed to go his own way, which does not differ in essentials from that of other ne'er-do-weels. He is no longer to be reckoned with as a possible claimant at Inayatullah's accession. One other there is who, if any credence may be given to the tales of Kabuli merchants in Peshawar, is causing Habibullah a succession of *mauvais quarts d'heure.* The Shahgassi Mulki, Sirdar Yahya Khan, the brother of the first Queen, who was driven from Afghanistan by Abdurrahman, has now been back in Afghanistan for about four years. Saving Nasrullah's priestly following, he commands the sympathy, so 'tis said, of all the tribes to the south and east of Kabul The Ghilzais, moreover, are known to have procured many rifles during the recent gun-running, and, inspired by the knowledge that they are well armed, have been showing signs of restlessness; whilst only the other day the Amir despatched the Hazrat Sahib Charbagh (one of the disciples of the well-known Hadda Mulla) to pacify the Sangu Khel, a Shinwari clan in the vicinity of Jellalabad, which had become intractable.

So long as Nasrullah retains his position at the head of the mullas he has nothing to fear. As a Durani, he evidently prefers to pull together with Habibullah than to risk the loss to his family of the legacy of subject tribes — Hazaras, Kafirs, Ghilzais, Usbegs, and Turcomans—that Abdurrahman bequeathed to the present Amir as the independent kingdom of Afghanistan, a kingdom that requires a firm hand if the unruly elements of which it is composed are to be held together.

Vexed by internal movements and hampered by the Anglophobe party in his dealings with us, the position of the Amir is certainly not an enviable one, nor is the administration of the country all that can be desired. What government there is in Afghanistan is conducted in the most haphazard fashion—at least, in the outlying districts, which for the most part are farmed out to governors or "hakims." The collection of the revenue is usually deferred to some two years after the expiry of their terms of office, when the hakims receive a summons to Kabul, and the major portion of their property is unceremoniously confiscated to supply the deficits in the exchequer. Corruption is rife. Under these circumstances it is not to be wondered at that the affairs of remote districts do not always come to the notice of the central Government as promptly as might be desired, in spite of the fact that in 1906 telephonic communication was established between Kabul and the principal provincial capitals. In many instances the first intimation of disorderly conduct on the part of his subjects reaches the Amir through the Government of India.

In this way Habibullah has made out a very plausible case for himself, and the sympathetic British lion has been within an ace of being caught napping. To all outward appearances, the Amir is merely an Oriental monarch, bound to Great Britain by certain treaty obligations, which he is honestly trying to fulfil, even at the risk of the allegiance of his subjects. He hears with regret (from the Government of India) that raids into British territory are being made from his side the Durand line. He replies that he has not yet been informed of the matter by his own officials, but that he will do all in his power to put an end to the raiding. He receives jirgas in Kabul, and, true to his engagements, he counsels them against any unfriendly attitude towards the British. They are then handed over to the chief imam. . . . He forbids the sale of rifles and ammunition to the independent tribes, but not the smallest attention is paid to this injunction. He pays a friendly visit to the Viceroy in India, where we are careful to inform him that we only wish to consolidate his position in his own kingdom, and to see Afghanistan able to defend herself. He accepts our assurances of friendship, and the howitzers presented to him by Lord Curzon, some of which, metaphorically, he mounts pointing towards Russia, some towards India. He spends the "allowance" granted to him on the defences of the Khurd Kabul Pass, and as soon as we propose building, as an earnest of our defensive treaty of alliance, a railway that shall facilitate the throwing of troops into Afghanistan in the event of a foreign invasion, he bares his teeth. Even while Sir Louis Dane was yet in Kabul, it was known in India that the Mission of 1905 was a complete fiasco. The proposals we had to make, according to the *Times* of January 26, 1905—the linking up of Peshawar and Jellalabad by rail and telegraph, the training of Afghan troops by British officers, the purchase of war material from England alone—Habibullah refused to discuss, substituting in their place Nasrullah's pet scheme, advocated as far back as 1897, during the latter's visit to England, for a legation in London which should transact business with the India Office over the head of the Viceroy, and an even more impossible request for a strip of land to the Baluch coast for the purpose of founding an Afghan seaport. Other instances could be cited for illustrating the insincerity of the Amir's professions, notably his obstructive policy with regard to the Mohmand Boundary Commission. As to the clauses affecting Afghanistan in the Anglo-Russian Agreement of 1907, the Amir has not yet signified his assent to them.

Utilizing every excuse that can be urged in extenuation of the Amir's attitude towards us, it can hardly be claimed that we have succeeded in making Afghanistan either a strong or a friendly kingdom. The very fact of our requiring a friendly attitude on the part of the Amir only contributes to his unpopularity among his subjects, and is one of the causes of his weak government.

Realizing all this, as he must, it is only natural that he should do something to reinstate himself in the eyes of his people. He is no longer content to remain merely the buffer State between Great Britain and Russia, and, with the intention of making himself altogether independent of Great Britain, it is not likely that he should despise the weapon that lies readiest to his hand in the shape of the impressionable independent border tribes, who are only too ready to follow his lead as long as we refrain from making our power felt.

CHAPTER IV

THE AUTUMN CRISIS, 1910

BEFORE proceeding to an account of the crisis of September and October, 1910, on the frontier, it will be necessary to trace briefly the rise of the arms traffic in the Persian Gulf.

Up till the year 1897—that is to say, the year of the great revolt in Tirah—the trade in arms through Muscat and Bushire had been chiefly confined to Persia and the countries at the head of the Gulf and on its southern shores. As "guardians of the Gulf" we had done what lay in our power to put a stop to this traffic. In 1891 we had been instrumental in inducing the Sultan of Muscat to prohibit the importation of arms into Gwadar and its dependencies, over which he lays a claim of suzerainty. In 1892 we were successful in obtaining a similar undertaking from the trucial chiefs of the Pirate Coast. For many years, however, Bushire continued to absorb the greater part of the trade, and the arming of the Bakhtiari tribesmen in the mountainous south-western corner of Persia went on apace. At the same time we may be sure that large quantities of rifles found their way into the possession of the semi-independent nomad tribes of the Arabian interior, especially among those chiefs who feared the aggressive designs of their powerful neighbour, Turkey.

After the Afridi revolt of 1897, the course of trade in arms veered round to the North-West Frontier, and large numbers of rifles began gradually to filter in, replacing the obsolete and home-made "jezail" with which the Afridis had hitherto for the most part been armed. It was at about this time that the Sultan of Muscat issued a proclamation granting to British and Persian men-of-war the power to search in Muscat waters vessels flying the flags of the three countries. The first-fruits of this agreement was the capture by H.M.S. *Lapwing* of 220 cases of arms and ammunition, destined for Bushire, on board the Anglo-Persian Steam Navigation Company's s.s. *Baluchistan*. The shippers afterwards hailed the Sultan and British Government into court, but on appeal to the House of Lords the principle on which the captain of the *Lapwing* had acted was upheld, and a verdict was returned in favour of the defendants. But in spite of this blow to the arms traffic, at least as far as it concerned Persia, by 1902 the trade through Persian and British Baluchistan had assumed such proportions that the Political Agent, Kalat, felt it his duty to come to some arrangement with the Governor-General of Kerman with a view to putting some check upon the traffic, which was already threatening the preservation of law and order on the Perso-Baluch frontier. It had, in fact, been found necessary in 1901 to send an expedition into Mekran to dislodge certain outlaws under Mahmud Khan, a noted ringleader, who for some time past had been committing raids into British territory from the security of several Baluch forts in the districts of Sarhad and Saravan. In a conversation with the Political Agent, Kalat, the Governor-General of Kerman agreed to issue a notification forbidding the further importation of arms along the coast of Persian Mekran, and to hold the Baluch Sardars responsible for any infringement of this regulation.

Thus far it might be thought that everything had been done to put an end to the traffic. But the authority of the Governor-General of Kerman, and even of the Deputy-Governor of Bampur, is, and always has been, of such a legendary character that little or no attention was paid to the notification by the Baluch Sardars, who are the real masters of this portion of the Persian dominions. The arms traffic continued to flourish in uninterrupted prosperity, and in spite of the repeated warnings of the Political Agent, Kalat, and, as time went on, of other frontier officers farther north, the gravity of the situation was not realized.

At the same time, in justice to the Government, it must be said that an attempt had been made in about 1900 to obtain the consent of France to the abrogation of the treaties which permitted the use of Muscat as an entrepôt for the arms traffic, and which allowed France to grant her flag to certain protégés in the port of Sur, under cover of which it was feared that nakhudas were enabled to evade search while running guns into Mekran.

With regard to the first point, it may as well be said at once that, short of a substantial cession of colonial territory to France*—an act against which sentiment revolts—or of the possession of some powerful diplomatic lever which chance may put into our hand, we shall never secure the abrogation of the trading treaties.

With regard to the second point, it was adjudged by the Hague tribunal in 1905 that "after January 2, 1892, France was not entitled to authorize vessels belonging to subjects of H.H. the Sultan of Muscat to fly the French flag," except on condition that their "owners or fitters-out had established, or should establish, that they had been considered and treated by France as her protégés before the year 1863," though "owners of dhows who before 1892 had been authorized by France to fly the French flag retained this authorization as long as France renewed it to the grantee."

It was not till the year 1907 that the undoubted truth of the warnings was brought home to the Government of India, in a manner which could not be ignored. In this year one big load of 30,000 rifles was successfully run through to Kandahar. It is said that a year or so previous to this, the

* A West African colony has been suggested.

Governments of New Zealand and New South Wales had had occasion to dispose of a quantity of old Government rifles which had seen service in the South African War. The purchaser seems to have been a man of no little enterprise. It boots not to inquire into the Homeric wanderings of these rifles between the date of their departure from the Antipodes and the date when the first of them reached the hands of one of the political officers on the North-West Frontier. Suffice it to say that the rifle was forwarded to Simla, where it seems to have been regarded as a very interesting curiosity—interesting enough, at all events, to be forwarded again to the India Office.

Further inquiries showed to what extent the danger on the frontier had grown, and Colonel Malleson was detailed on special duty to report on the traffic through Afghanistan to the North-West Frontier. The result of his report was to convince the Government of India that no time should be lost in instituting measures of the most repressive kind. Military operations, which were undertaken at Robat, were found inadequate to the situation in view of the nature of the country over which watch had to be kept. A Gurkha battalion was, however, stationed there in case of eventualities, which succeeded in making several important captures. Accordingly, in 1909 a rigorous blockade was instituted in the Persian Gulf and in the Gulf of Oman. During the cold-weather season of 1909-10 so numerous were the captures of gun-running dhows that the Arab skippers soon learnt to look before they "skipped."

And now we come to the genesis of the autumn crisis of last year on the frontier. Before the development of the arms traffic through Afghanistan, what rifles were in the possession of the Pathans had either been run in through British India or were the products of successful rifle-stealing from regimental guard-houses. Of some 1,500 rifles returned at the end of the Tirah campaign, the majority were identified as having been stolen in this manner. Coffins had also been successfully employed to convey rifles across the frontier under the very eyes of unsuspecting militia patrols. In Calcutta rifles had been strapped under goods-waggons destined for Peshawar, whence they were secretly carried off by natives on arrival. Ammunition had gone through the Khaibar cleverly concealed in bales of merchandise. Bolts had disappeared mysteriously from arms-racks. All these methods of obtaining arms now suffered a severe slump. It was no longer worth while stabbing a sentry in the back to get his rifle. The cunning which had prompted the rifle-thief in the stillness of the night to pitch a pebble to one side of a sentry and to attack him from the other while his attention was distracted in the direction of the sound was no longer called forth. These ways were too difficult and dangerous, and were not always rewarded with success.

Even the Adam Khel Afridis who owned rifle-factories in the Kohat Pass began to appreciate the decline in trade consequent on the appearance of the "vilayeti" (European) rifle with which the border was being inundated. The "pass-made" rifle fell in price to half its value. With one accord the Adam Khel closed their workshops and invested in the new avenue of trade. A few went themselves to the Gulf, but the majority entrusted their savings to the Powindah merchants who now visited Mekran in large numbers. These Powindahs, it is said, were financed in some cases by the Amir, on condition the rifles were sold in districts designated by him.

For a time everything went well. Rifles poured into the frontier. But suddenly the crash came. The Pathans who, returning from Mekran, reached their homes about the beginning of June, 1910, reported that they had been unable to obtain rifles. The ships of the "Sirkar," they said, had put an end to the trade. Their money was in the hands of the dealers in Muscat.

Whole clans were ruined—nay, whole tribes. All through the summer indignation grew. Raiding recommenced with unexampled persistence. Demands from tribes-people for compensation began to be heard. The Adam Khel reopened their workshops, on the principle that "'tis an ill wind that blows nobody any good." It was of no avail; nobody had any money wherewith to buy even a "pass-made" rifle.

But though the suppression of gun-running in

the Persian Gulf had undoubtedly had its full provocative effect on the tribes of the North-West Frontier, yet there had not been wanting causes of unrest, which, independently of gun-running and, to all appearances, of each other, had been gradually leading up to a frontier crisis. Gun-running in its succeeding phases, first of toleration and then of suppression by Government, had provided first the means and then the pretext for a rising. In a sense, then, it should be regarded more as the latest development in the situation than as the *fons et origo* of all the trouble.

That an outburst was, at least for the time being, warded off reflects the highest credit on the tact and judgment of the frontier political officers. For not since 1897 had such a favourable opportunity for combined action occurred simultaneously all along the frontier. In nearly every quarter disaffection had been rife. Not only in the south had the Mulla Powindah, since 1904 the evil genius of the Waziri border, been exerting himself in the cause of Islam, but in the north, in Swat and Bajaur, the Gud Mulla, upon whom fell the mantle of the late Hadda Mulla, had also, in a tentative manner, taken up his parable. At the same time, there was evidence that influences of Afghan origin had been at work to seduce the tribes-people from their allegiance—influences which seemed to point to the fact that a rising of the independent tribes would not have been looked upon with disfavour in certain quarters in Kabul.

Yet further signs of the times were to be found in the revived activity of the Hindustani fanatics, a politico-religious sect which for twenty years had been practically regarded as a cipher in Indian politics. What passed between Nasrullah and Abdul Kerim, the nephew of their present leader, during the latter's visit to Kabul in the autumn of last year has not yet transpired, but it is safe to say that it bodes no good to us, and we shall probably hear of them again before very long.

But by far the most dangerous exhibition of ill-feeling came from the Khaibar Afridis, and especially among the Zakka Khel section, who saw in the disaffection of the Kohat Pass Afridis an opportunity not to be lost of forwarding their own quarrel with the Government of India.

As in 1897 and in 1908, so to-day the tribes on the Peshawar border take their cue from this powerful division of the Afridis; and it is as much due to the fact that the Khaibar Afridis hesitated to take the lead as to anything else that the Kohat Pass Afridis, who of all the tribes had suffered most in connection with the suppression of the gun-running, acquiesced in the refusal of Government to compensate them for their losses.

A word as to the divisions of the Afridis. The Afridis themselves are divided into three great divisions distinct from one another. These are—(1) the Khaibar Afridis; (2) the Adam Khel or Kohat Pass Afridis; (3) the Aka Khel Afridis.

Though participants in the Afridi rising of 1897.

taking a prominent part in the burning of Landi Kotal and Ali Masjid, the Aka Khel have given us little trouble in comparison with the other sections of the Afridis. Owing to their geographical position midway between the Khaibar and Kohat Passes, when in 1881 allowances were apportioned to the Afridi clans for the policing of these passes, the Aka Khel found themselves excluded. They remained, therefore, for many years the only tribe among the Afridis not in receipt of Government grants. This has constituted their chief grievance, venting itself in numerous petty raids into British territory. To remedy this very natural feeling of jealousy, a pretext was found for granting them an allowance, and in 1902 they were entrusted with the protection of their section of the frontier. Since that year they have not shown any active hostility. They are, however, in the habit of harbouring outlaws, as it is contrary to their code of honour to give up anyone taking refuge among them, and for this they have been fined more than once. Notable among these refugees was the Hazarnao gang, which in recent years, from the safe retreat of the hills between the Bara River and the Kohat Pass, committed many raids on the Peshawar district.

The Adam Khel, who live in the mountainous district between Peshawar and Kohat, through which for fifteen miles runs the Kohat Pass, are, as has been mentioned before, the only section of the Afridis who show any capacity for trade.

THE KHAIBAR PASS.

SOME AFRIDI TYPES.

They are engaged in carrying salt, and also in the manufacture of rifles, for the production of which there are half a dozen workshops in the pass owned by the Galai section of the Afridis. They have no connection with either the Aka Khel or the Khaibar Afridis, and are politically under the Deputy-Commissioner, Kohat.

The Khaibar Afridis are further divided into six clans, which I here, for the sake of convenience, tabulate under their respective political factions of Samil and Gar, the origin and meaning of which are lost in the mists of antiquity, but whose ramifications extend to all the tribes between the Khaibar and Kurram. Like Whig and Tory, the Afridi accepts, as a matter of course, the traditions of the faction to which he is born. As Samil or Gar, *nascitur, non fit.*

Samil.	Gar.
Malikdin Khel.	Kambar Khel.
Zakka Khel.	Kuki Khel.
Sipahs.	Kamrai.

There is a dynastic alliance between the Malikdin Khel and the Kambar Khel, while the Zakka Khel and the Kuki Khel are mortal enemies. The Sipahs and Kamrai are of minor importance. These clans live in Tirah in the summer, coming down in winter to the country along the south of the Khaibar Pass, and are therefore known as "do-kora," or "two-homes." To these clans, from whom are recruited the Khaibar Rifles, is entrusted the guarding of the pass, for which services they receive allowances amounting to the value of the tolls levied by them before the British occupation of the pass. There is no more mistaken idea than to regard these allowances as a kind of danegeld, by which it is hoped to buy off raiders from making inroads into the Peshawar district. Such a policy would only serve to aggravate the evil.

The tranquillity of the passes and the consequent rapid growth of trade has tended to enrich the tribes-people, who can now come and go with greater security and regularity in pursuit of their own humble trade, which for the most part consists in carrying firewood into Peshawar. This enhanced prosperity, far from having had any marked civilizing effect, seems rather to have rendered increasingly difficult the task of the maliks in keeping order among the more unruly element. Moreover, one or two successful raids, for which reparation was not immediately exacted, had still further increased the arrogance of the tribes-people.

After the Zakka Khel Expedition of 1908, each of the Afridi clans, by the terms of the agreement then come to, undertook responsibility for the good behaviour of one section of the Zakka Khel. This was never meant to be a permanent measure by those who made it, nor did the Zakka Khel, who consider themselves a match for any two of the other clans, contemplate an indefinite submission to the yoke of their neighbours, even had these latter felt themselves capable of enforcing it.

For ten years there has been a bitter blood-feud

between the Zakka Khel and the Kuki Khel, which from time to time breaks out with more than usual ferocity. At such times it is the obvious duty of the other clans, under the agreement of 1908, to intervene and put a stop to this internecine strife. But here the eternal question of Samil and Gar crops up to divide the Afridi jirga among itself, and to destroy the balance of power in this tumultuous commonwealth. The Malikdin Khel, being in politics Samil, refuse to take sides against the Zakka Khel, and the Kambar Khel, though of the Gar faction, hold to the Malikdin Khel on account of their common ancestry. The two remaining clans, conscious of their numerical inferiority, are too frightened to exhibit any active sympathies.

When roused, there is no saying to what lengths the Afridi will go, and these internal feuds constitute a direct menace to the security of the pass, and thus violate the agreements of 1881 and 1908, by which the trade through the passes is safeguarded and the tranquillity of the Zakka Khel guaranteed. Any infringement of these undertakings renders punitive intervention not only legitimate but almost obligatory.

In the midst of these internal dissensions, the news of their losses as the result of the suppression of the gun-running raised the indignation of the Zakka Khel to fever-heat, and the Afridi clans, all of whom had been affected in a greater or less degree, were found either unwilling or powerless to restrain them. At the same time, the demand made to Government by the Kohat Pass Afridis for compensation, which received a firm refusal, led to the perpetration of numerous raids into the Peshawar district, and the mail-tonga was held up and looted in the Kohat Pass, which was in consequence closed for about a fortnight in September.

At one time in September it looked as if hostilities could hardly be avoided. The situation had resolved itself into the problem of how long the Kambar and Malikdin Khel would remain content with merely evincing a passive sympathy towards the turbulent Zakkas. There were even budmashes among the Kuki Khel prepared to sink their feud in order to foment a general Zakka Khel rising against the British. Excited by the success of several raids at this time, the warlike spirit of the Zakka Khel threatened to obliterate the memory of the expedition of 1908. As a precaution a guard was placed on the bridges over the Indus at Attock and Kushalgurh, both of which are threatened from the low hills of the Jowaki Afridi country. But chiefly owing to the tactful treatment of the situation by Mr. Merk, acting as Chief Commissioner in the absence of Sir George Roos-Keppel, the storm was happily averted, though it was some time before it could be said that the frontier had returned to its normal degree of tranquillity. However, it may be hoped that a final and satisfactory termination has resulted from the deliberations of a united Afridi jirga held by Sir George Roos-Keppel in Peshawar on December 3, at which all parties were fully represented, and in which it was tacitly agreed to drop the question of losses sustained, since it was obvious that there was no intention on the part of the Government to comply with their request.

CHAPTER V

TRIBAL RESPONSIBILITY VERSUS FANATICISM

ONCE again, therefore, the priming of the Pathan pistol has been followed by a flash in the pan. The whole history of the frontier has been made up of such abortive attempts at revolt, with here and there an interval of short-lived success. But though the Pathan is capable of causing the despatch of a considerable quantity of cipher telegrams, these sporadic outbursts are mere side-shows, and in reality there is an unmarked struggle going on all the time for the sovereignty over this no-man's-land which we call the independent territory. Western diplomacy is being pitted against Oriental finesse, and the commercial instinct is being employed to exorcise the militant spirit of Islam. The wire-pullers in this little comedy are the Amir on the one hand and the Government of India on the other, and the marionettes at the end of the wires are respectively the mullas and the maliks or tribal headmen.

The problem with which the Government of India is now confronted is that of convincing the maliks, and through them the bulk of the tribes-people, that it is useless any longer to kick against the pricks, and that in lending an ear to the fantastic schemes of the mullas for driving the infidel beyond the Indus they are only laying up for themselves retribution in the near future, instead of the treasure in heaven which they so fondly imagine.

By no other means will the Pathans be induced to combine in any definite action with a view to putting down raiding or expelling firebrands from their borders. As a race they are too intensely democratic, and concerted action between the members of even a small subsection of a tribe only arises from two motives—one of which is religious fanaticism, the other self-interest. The former being a monopoly of the Moslem inhabitants, there remains but the latter to Government for the accomplishment of its object. Once, then, that this idea of self-interest, of material benefit, of something to be gained and of something to be lost, is aroused in the minds of the tribal elders, a powerful counter-agent begins to operate against and gradually to undermine the nefarious influence of the mullas.

The system that has been adopted for inculcating these ideas is known as that of "tribal responsibility," by which the lawlessness of this people is gradually giving way before the better instincts of more civilized communities—industry, discipline, and respect for property and authority. Thus, the maliks are responsible for the repair and policing of the roads through their territories, protection of the border, keeping open the passes, prevention of raiding, expulsion of outlaws from their borders, restitution of stolen property, etc., for all of which services they receive allowances in proportion to their value to the State. These allowances can always be, and frequently are, stopped when the tribe proves incapable of fulfilling its obligations; and this system has been found to work well, especially among the Afridis, who, besides not being so susceptible to the wiles of the mullas, have a certain *flair* for the buttered side of the bread. This was well illustrated in the Zakka Khel Expedition of 1908, when the Afridi maliks evinced no desire to risk the loss of their allowances by allowing the clans under their charge to join in the fray.

In spite of their constitutional hostility towards us, the Pathans show a decided readiness to enlist in the frontier militias, which, since the reincorporation of the Punjab Frontier Force with the regular army, have been raised in most of the agencies. These are the Chitral Scouts, Khaibar Rifles, Kurram Militia, Northern and Southern Waziristan Militias, forming a force of some 14,000 troops directly under the command of the Chief Commissioner of the North-West Frontier Province. These native militias render invaluable service in intercepting raiding-parties, but, in spite of their extreme mobility in this respect, it is obviously impossible for them to be on the actual spot selected by the raiders as their objective, unless previous information has been received, and in the case of villages near the border it is easy for the raiders to make a sudden descent and to carry off their booty to the hills long before the militia-men can arrive to intercept them.

To remedy this evil the somewhat risky experiment was made last year of rearming* the headmen of those border villages on whose loyalty it was felt we could depend. There is, of course, always the chance of these rifles being used against us in the future; but it is not unnatural that tribes within our border, and entitled to our protection, should consider as rather illogical a situation in which, while debarred from seeking satisfaction in the way most congenial to them—*i.e.*, by making counter-raids—they were compelled to submit to systematic plundering without the means even of offering an effective resistance.

One of the greatest obstacles that has stood in the way of the extension of this system among the tribes is the fact that in some cases the maliks have contracted responsibilities which, owing to the democratic spirit of the Pathans, they have since found themselves unable to discharge. This is especially the case among the Mahsuds of Southern Waziristan, who, besides being inveterate raiders and more than usually susceptible to fanatical influences, are democratic to such a degree that the term "malik," as applied to a

* Lord Curzon had caused the disarmament of the border villages.

Mahsud, is a ridiculous misnomer. The assembly known as the Mahsud jirga practically includes the whole tribe. The agreement come to at the termination of the Mahsud blockade was signed by no fewer than 1,565 so-called maliks, each of whom considered his personal participation in the proceedings indispensable.

From this democratic condition it follows that the richer, and, on this account, presumably more influential, maliks are not necessarily those best able to preserve order. Those maliks, in fact, who annually received the tribal allowances were, in many cases, found quite incapable of controlling the ruck of the tribe. Their influence over the younger members was *nil*, and it was found repeatedly necessary to fine them and to stop their allowances.

As *agents provocateurs* of the Kabul Anglophobe party, the mullas naturally head the anti-malik faction, and in a country where the inhabitants are steeped in the grossest superstition, even the mullas themselves being in most cases ignorant of the true doctrines of the religion they profess to teach, it is not to be expected that their hold over the population will be easily loosened. In spite of the fact that in the Mahommedan religion there are, properly speaking, no priests, the whole country is overrun by an hereditary hierarchy of mendicant fanatics—hereditary as being composed of Saiyids, or descendants of the Prophet, and Sahibs, or descendants of the "associates" of the Prophet, with their innumerable following of "murids," or disciples. For all of these the tribes-people have the profoundest reverence, and their graves are, after death, places of pilgrimage and the scenes of reputed miracles, which often take the form of the grave growing longer as the saintly reputation of its occupant increases. One of these, situated in Peshawar Cantonment itself, and known as the "nau-gajar," or nine-yarder, attained to such a length that it threatened to grow right across the road. One night, however, the cantonment magistrate ordained that a wall should be built round it, since when it has been kept more or less within reasonable bounds. These "ziarats," or shrines, are held in such respect that the natives, on leaving their homes for any length of time, do not hesitate to deposit their household valuables near one of them, in the full certainty of finding them there on their return. Shrines are frequently erected over the bodies of Musalmans who have died fighting against the "unbeliever," and it is not uncommon to see several of these within a short distance of, and sometimes right under, the walls of a British fort. At Jandola, in Southern Waziristan, there is one actually in the barbed-wire entanglements that surround the fort. It is considered a dishonour for a clan not to possess one or more of these shrines; and it is related of the Zakka Khel that, being on this account an object of contempt among the other Afridi clans they one day induced an exceptionally holy man to visit them, whom they promptly murdered, thus wiping away the stain on their honour, and at the same time acquiring a shrine which soon became the envy of the surrounding countryside.

Independent territory is divided by a belt of comparatively non-fanatical tribes—a circumstance which explains to a great extent the difficulty the mullas experience in organizing a simultaneous rising all over the frontier. Southern Waziristan is fanatical, and the whole of the Peshawar border north of the Khaibar (Swat, Bajaur, Buner, Agror, and the Mohmands) intensely so. Tirah and the Kurram, however, are little influenced by the fiery exhortations of the mullas, and though Tirah is potentially our most formidable enemy on the frontier, it chooses its own time for a hostile demonstration, and refuses to dance to the piping of every wandering faqir. The following will illustrate this trait of the Afridis: During the Mohmand rising of 1908 the Sufi Sahib of Batikot, through jealousy of the Hazrat Sahib of Charbagh, retired from the Mohmand country, and entered Tirah, with the intention of raising a lashkar there. He gave out that he had the power of turning bullets into water. In any other portion of the frontier this statement would have been accorded full credence, but the Afridis were not born yesterday. They suggested that he should first give an exhibition of these powers, deciding that the trial should be carried out on his own person. As was to be expected, the mulla did not care to risk his skin in this manner, and was hooted out of Tirah.

It is this non-conducting area that has for so long frustrated the efforts of the mullas to bring about a combined revolt against British rule, and a point on which it is impossible to lay too much stress is that Tirah is the KEYSTONE of the whole situation. As in 1897, so to-day, the revolt of Tirah would be the signal for a general rising of all the Pathan tribes. But as long as Tirah remains passive, so long will the efforts of the mullas in the more fanatical districts resemble the explosions of damp gunpowder.

Before the conclusion of the Durand Agreement the Pathans feared the Amir's designs on their independence no less than our own, and even accused him of being the friend of the "infidel"; but now that their freedom has been guaranteed from attack on that side, they look on the Amir as their natural ally. Even now the frontier from Mount Sikaram, the western extremity of the Sofaid Koh, to the Nawa Kotal in Bajaur remains undemarcated, chiefly owing to the dilatory and obstructive policy of the Amir, who was astute enough to recognize the value of such an open door into our back-yard, which might be utilized by his emissaries without incurring any responsibility for interfering in affairs on our side of the line. Little troubles are constantly cropping up on the frontier below Landi Kotal, and the undemarcated portion of the Mohmand boundary is a continual source of danger, as the territory to which it gives access is a veritable hotbed of fanaticism and intrigue. For half a century it has harboured the political riffraff of North-West India—the Sitana or Hindustani fanatics, the mutinous 55th Native Infantry Regiment in 1857, the Hadda Mulla and his successors, the Gud (Lame) Mulla and the Sufi Sahib, the Hazrat Sahib and the Mad Faqir (known also as the Mulla Mastan or the Sartor Faqir)—and the Mohmand tribe, half of which is Afghan and half independent, surges backward and forward at will, and Afghan lashkars infringe the Durand Agreement with impunity.

Whatever measure of success may be said to have attended Abdurrahman's treatment of the "jehad" (holy war) question, he certainly never succeeded in organizing the frontier priesthood as the Amir's brother, Nasrullah, has done. Not only has the latter been successful in reconciling to each other many who formerly were enemies through jealousy of each other's influence or sect, but he has created a regular network by which communication is kept up between the northern and southern parts of the province, and these in turn are in communication with Kabul.

Formerly the activities of the mullas had been centred on their own narrow and selfish little interests. The preservation of their own saintly reputations and the undermining, by fair means or foul, of the reputation of any rival divine, varied by an occasional jehad, seemed in their eyes a praiseworthy aim and object. Many a plot directed against the British failed through the petty jealousies of its authors. Few of them were capable of such patriotism as the late Akhund of Swat, who, in spite of religious differences of opinion, used his influence on behalf of his rival, Saiyid Akbar Shah, the leader of the Sitana fanatics, to procure his election as King of Swat, at a time when the proximity of the British demanded, and the rivalry between the Swatis deferred, the choice of a recognized leader. Few, like him, had the good sense to perceive that the independence of Swat was more easily preserved by adopting a friendly attitude towards us than by continual raiding into British territory.

The reasons that have led Nasrullah to stir up the mullas to a sense of their common interests are to be found in the general belief, entertained all over the Mahommedan world, that the European nations contemplate a partition of the entire Islamic area that yet retains a semblance of freedom in Western Asia. Events in Turkey, Egypt, Morocco, Arabia, and Persia, are followed with anxious interest. Close touch is maintained with the Pan-Islamic League. These fears receive daily confirmation in the rumours of proposed railway construction across Persia, and the discussions about respective spheres of influence that are carried on in a cool proprietary tone in the newspapers. Moreover, the advent of civilization and education in these countries spells loss of influence to the mullas, whose power varies in direct proportion to the credulity of the masses. Thus the mullas are fighting not only for their religion, but for their daily bread.

Appearances being decidedly against the European nations, Nasrullah has not hesitated to enlist the active co-operation of every sect, not even despising the exiguous remnant of the once formidable body of fanatical warriors known as the Hindustani or Sitana fanatics. These at one time had made themselves masters of the whole of Yusufzai and Peshawar, but on the arrival of the British west of the Indus were hunted from pillar to post, until they finally found refuge among the Amazais of the Black Mountain, where they have remained since 1888, in spite of a treaty by which the Amazais undertook to expel them from their borders. The elaboration of this scheme was materially assisted by a "ghaza," or Church Congress, which Nasrullah caused to be summoned for the discussion of these and kindred matters, and secret agents have been appointed for the maintenance of close relations with such outlying districts as Southern Waziristan. For this purpose Khost is found to be a very convenient halfway house, since it is within easy reach of the Mulla Powindah and the Hamzullah Mulla, and the Khostwals can always be counted upon to assist in attacks on the Shias of the Kurram Valley.* The mullas of Ningrahar, who are both

* Lala Pir and the Malang Faqir collected a lashkar here in 1908, to be used against the Shias.

influential and numerous, devote themselves to intrigue in Tirah and the country to the north of the Khaibar.

Of the more remote tribes inhabiting the valleys on either side of the Chitral Road, in Upper Swat and the vast tract known as Kohistan, little is known, and the Government of India rarely comes into contact with them, except indirectly through the Nawab of Dir. The strategic value of Chitral vanished with the cessation of the Russian advance in the Pamirs and the conclusion of the labours of the Pamir Boundary Commission, which interposed the narrow strip of Afghan territory, known as Wakhan, between the rival empires. But, in spite of its dangerous isolation, it is thought advisable to retain a hold on this distant outpost, owing to the difficulty of getting into the country again should the necessity arise. The yearly reliefs go up in October, and from that time onwards the little garrison is cut off from British territory by 100 odd miles of treacherous country and two difficult passes. A railway runs from Naushera to Dargai, at the mouth of the Malakand Pass, and the Malakand movable column is ever ready to secure the line of communications. The security of the road is, however, continually menaced by the constant intertribal fighting that goes on between the Nawab of Dir and his son, Mian Gul Jan. The signal services and thorough loyalty of the Nawab for many years past have always been gratefully recognized, and, indeed, it is very fortunate that such a large portion of the independent territory should be in the hands of a ruler who is known to discourage the presence of hot-gospellers in his territories. Quite recently (December, 1910) the subject-tribes in the Upper Swat Valley, who pay him a yearly tribute, threw off their allegiance, drove the Nawab's tax-gatherers from the country, and prepared to offer a spirited resistance to the collection of the revenue. The Nawab immediately collected a lashkar, and, unaided by any outside help, soon regained control over his unruly subjects.

Meanwhile, in other parts of the province, in spite of occasional set-backs, the tribes-people are gradually being brought to realize the wisdom of following the line of least resistance. Every year fresh evidence is forthcoming to show that the policy of imposing responsibility on the maliks for the behaviour of the tribes under their charge is one that has been justified by results, and perhaps the greatest proof of this is to be found in the peaceful termination of the crisis through which we have just passed.

CHAPTER VI

FROM PESHAWAR TO PARACHINAR

THE enormous mountain massif of Tirah, forming the keystone of the frontier arch, runs down between the Peshawar and Kohat borders to within fifteen miles of the Indus, neatly halving the province. Its eastern extremity is known as the country of the Jowaki Afridis, and as such is cut off from Tirah proper by the Kohat Pass, which connects Peshawar and Kohat. The Jowaki Afridis, like the Galai Afridis, who inhabit the pass, are a section of the large tribe of the Adam Khel Afridis.

It was through this pass that I found myself careering along one December morning at full gallop in a dak-tonga on my way to Kohat, *en route* for the Kurram Valley and Parachinar. We had left Peshawar at half-past ten, and, skirting the southern wall of the city, past where the "lungi"-weavers prepare and dye the long woof of cotton which eventually becomes a turban, through the long avenues of bul-bul trees and the slow-moving throng of bullock-carts, buffaloes, donkeys, camels, and other beasts of burden, with their attendant drivers, had at last reached the open plain. Kohat is forty miles off, and we hoped to do the journey in four hours. The first stage of about seven miles took us fully an hour, and the fresh pair of horses jibbed at starting. This happened also at the second change, and at the third the sluggish "near" horse lay down in the dust, breaking his harness, or rather its string fastenings. When the tonga-wallah had induced it to resume a perpendicular position once more by stamping with an iron-shod boot on its nose (I made feeble expostulations in English), more string was produced, and we started off at a wild gallop. At Matanni post we changed horses again, and the shaft-horse jibbed anew. It is always the shaft-horse that jibs. The "off" horse. "tied" to the tonga with some string and a leather trace, seldom gives trouble, unless by backing out into the road at right angles to the shaft-horse, and outside his trace. Sometimes both horses are harnessed to a pole, with a kind of iron yoke, which clanks and clatters when they gallop in step. But when galloping out of step, the natural oscillation of their bodies keeps the yoke always fast against the pole, and the noiseless seesaw, seesaw of the yoke goes on like the pistons of a double-suction pump. Many of the tonga-horses seem to know this, and avoid the discordant clank, clatter, clank of the yoke. At Matanni we picked up a Subadar-Major of the Frontier Militia, on his way to Kohat, and with the aid of an interpreter he explained to me the topography of the pass.

We were then just entering the foot-hills of the Galai country, and from time to time we passed groups of tall and wild-looking Afridis, all armed with modern rifles, for we were now in independent territory. These looked askance at the white man, for they were under the displeasure of the Sirkar, having held up and looted several tongas during the disturbances that had occasioned the recall of the Chief Commissioner from England. A little farther on the narrow valley began to assume the appearance of a Scottish glen, with green fields of barley on either hand, and presently we drew up at a village of the Zarghun Khel, with its mud-walled, fort-like dwellings, its whitened "hujrah" or guest-house, and its "karkhana" or workshop (*i.e.*, rifle-factory). There are six or seven of these rifle-factories in different villages in the Adam Khel country, and though the rifles produced in them cannot compare with those run in from the Persian Gulf, yet a fairly brisk business is done, especially when the efforts of the blockading squadron in the Gulf have reduced competition. The chief difficulty that the Afridi workmen experience is in the rifling of the barrel and in the construction of the bolt, which accounts for the frequency with which in former years rifle-bolts disappeared in a mysterious manner from regimental arms-racks. It was with great regret that, owing to the strained relations which subsisted at the time between the Adam Khel and the Government, I was obliged to continue my journey without having paid a visit to the interior of one of these karkhanas.

For several miles more the road continued to wind through this narrow valley of low foot-hills, till of a sudden a sheer blank wall of rock blocked the end of the valley. Up the side of this wall we zigzagged, and presently reached Fort Mackeson at the summit, looking out both ways over the Kohat Plain and the valley through which we had just come. Far away through the haze we could make out the silver thread of the Kohat River as it wound its way eastward over the level plain. Below, on the right, and following the curve of the hillside, the white ribbon of road floated downwards like the "paying-off" pennon of a man-of-war. Away to the left a faint brown scar across the mountain-side showed where the ancient track of the Buddhist pilgrims of bygone centuries led northwards to the Himalaya.

At Kohat I put up for one night at the house of the Deputy-Commissioner, who was away on tour at the time. This bungalow was designed and built by the ill-fated Cavagnari, who was massacred in Kabul with all his followers during the second Afghan War. It possesses a central rotundo with a domed roof, round which the rooms are built, this design being adopted for the sake of coolness during the hot weather. The Revenue Commissioner's bungalow in Peshawar is built on the same plan, and as far as I know is the only other like it, being an exact replica. During my brief stay in

Kohat I was indebted for much kindness to Colonel and Mrs. Kennedy, and have grateful remembrance of the hospitality extended to me, and of a pleasant evening spent with them. Kohat is a delightfully cool and shady-looking place for a frontier cantonment, and its green foliage is in striking contrast to the barren semicircle of hills which close it in on the north and west. From rising ground on the outskirts of the cantonment may be seen the V-shaped notch in the hills through which the Ublan Pass leads up to the Miranzai border, rendered historic during the Afridi revolt of 1897. It was through here that the main southern advance into Tirah under General Lockhart took place.

Kohat lies on the narrow-gauge railway from Kushalgurh on the Indus, and it was along this railway that I continued my journey westward the next day to Thall, its terminus. The line follows the Miranzai border along the southern face of the Samana Ridge, on whose crest the two forts, Cavagnari and Lockhart, look down into Orakzai Tirah. These two forts are held by the Samana Rifles, a frontier militia raised from the surrounding tribes. At Hangu, the "jumping-off place" for the Samana Ridge, the little train was boarded by an army of locusts, in the shape of some fifty or sixty sepoys of the Kurram Militia, just returning from furlough to their regiment at Parachinar. As the train was already fairly full up, and there seemed no possibility of obtaining any more carriages, every available footboard and platform was soon covered with a yelling and writhing mass of beturbaned strap-hangers, shouting and gesticulating to their friends on distant portions of the train, and waving good-byes to their relations on the platform, which seemed as crowded as before. The journey from Kohat to Thall covers about sixty miles, and lasts nearly the whole day. Towards evening it was curious to see some devout Mahommedan spread his prayer-carpet on the platform and perform his evening devotions in the midst of the seething mob, wholly oblivious for the time to the discordancies of the world about him. Among this crowd may often be seen the Powindah or Kabuli merchants, on their way down into India. Their tattered clothes and dirty red-bearded faces give no indication of their means, and for all one can tell the most ruffianly among them may be on his way to Calcutta or Bombay. Sometimes they go even farther afield, to Australia and even British Columbia, where I have seen them employed in sawmills. The story goes that one day a British officer, whose motor-bicycle had broken down on the way up to Parachinar, was electrified on being accosted by a huge bearded Powindah with a "Why, hullo, son! what's wrong with the 'bike'?" Through the throng also move black-robed Turi women with covered faces, sturdy Afghan women with a jingling necklace and breastplate of Kabuli rupees; buxom, laughing Afridi wenches with their short kilts, and ever and anon the skirl of the "serenai"—the Pathan equivalent of the bagpipes—is heard above the incessant din.

The Kurram Valley lies immediately to the south of Tirah and the Orakzai country. Remarkable alike for the beauty of its scenery and for the friendly character of its inhabitants, it presents in this respect a marked contrast to the rest of the North-West Frontier Province. The entrance to the Kurram leads through a narrow and barren defile, commanded by the fort of Thall, which is situated on an eminence of great natural strength. Here I passed the night in the dak-bungalow, setting out early on the following morning through the narrow entrance to the valley, to the tune of the long-drawn, melancholy howl that the tonga-wallah extracts from his battered bugle as a warning to the natives of the approach of the mail-tonga.

A curious sight we must present to the sleepy-eyed Turi as he watches our approach through the cold dawn, with a letter or a parcel in his hand for the post. Strapped on either side over the wheels are two Peshauri mule-trunks, or "yakhdans," and two bundles of bedding. On the roof of the conveyance is a ragged and unkempt urchin, used for starting the ponies when they jib, tying the harness again when it breaks, and performing odd jobs of varying utility. Our Jehu is attired in a khaki militia great-coat, and wears a blue turban, the end of which is wound round his mouth to keep the dust out of his lungs. A pair of motor-goggles for the front passenger is not so much a luxury as a necessity. In this fashion we proceed till the mounting sun compels me to change my cap for a topee, to avoid sunstroke. Presently we stop at the village of Manduri, and I make the acquaintance of a hospitable custom of the Pathans. The headman of the village, Hamid Khan, presents himself, and, after the usual salutation, offers me a cup of tea. This is an invitation which cannot be refused without giving offence. The best tea-service is brought out—a very fine affair—and a charpoy to sit on, and for once the tea is excellent. It is not always so, but one cannot refuse, even though the sugar has been upset and picked out of the dust by grimy hands, as happened to me on one occasion.

After leaving Manduri the valley broadens out and the road sweeps up a gradual ascent to Sadda Post, some thirty-five miles from Thall, where the valley takes a sharp bend to the left. On either hand are diminutive fields surrounded by "bunds," or banks, for irrigation purposes. The fertile soil here produces two crops annually—wheat in winter and rice or Indian corn in summer. The fields descend in terraces to the Kurram River, which is perennially fed by the snowfields of the Sofaid Koh. Chenab-trees of great size and age afford a pleasant shade to the fortified villages, which everywhere present an appearance of prosperity not to be met with in the more arid parts of the province. These trees, as convenient rendezvous for raiders, have each a name by which they are known to the natives.

At Sadda Post I met the Political Agent for the Kurram, Mr. S. E. Pears, to whom I had a letter of introduction, and as he had come down from Parachinar on urgent matters of State, I decided to stay there with him a couple of days, and return with him to Parachinar. Sadda Post lies just to the south of the Chamkanni country, and has stood a siege more than once, notably in the rising of 1896. At the time when I was there the village was full of Massuhzai and Alisherzai clansmen of the Orakzai tribe, who, with numbers of Turis, had been summoned to appear in jirga before the Political Officer.

As most of the differences between the Government and the independent tribes are settled in this way, it may not be out of place to present to the reader a mental picture of one of the more orderly varieties of jirga.

With a view to creating as much trouble as possible, the maliks, or headmen, of the clan have turned up two days late, only to find that the Political Officer has gone off in his turn in another direction, apparently oblivious to this manœuvre on their part. In reality he had been expecting it. They are now, perforce, compelled to await his pleasure, or forfeit the small grant that Government generally makes towards their travelling expenses, which in the case of the more distant tribes is, to them, a matter of some importance. When the Political Officer returns, he finds that the tribe has come in in great force, scenting a day's feed at Government expense. All the "grey-beards" of the tribe are here, as well as many of the younger members, some armed, in number about 400. The scene presents a picture almost Biblical in its solemnity, the analogy being heightened by the Jewish type so prevalent among the Pathans.

Assisted by the Extra-Assistant-Commissioner, generally a Khan of good local family, the Political Officer takes his seat, the jirga disposes itself round him on the ground in a semicircle, and the discussion begins, graduating in violence according to the "jungliness" of the tribe. The case for settlement is as follows: The tribe in question has gone bail in Rs. 5,000 for the good behaviour of a notorious outlaw among their number. This outlaw has since raided a tribe under British protection, carried off much loot and several prisoners, and escaped through his own country into the back of beyond. The tribe is now faced with the knotty problem of rescuing the prisoners and re-capturing the outlaw, or of suffering the loss of Rs. 5,000. What, then, are they to do? In spite of having been badly let in by a "pal," their sympathies are all with the miscreant, whom they consider to have performed a very commendable feat. Had he not succeeded in escaping, their verdict would have been otherwise, and he would

TURIS OF THE KURRAM VALLEY.

ORAKZAI TRIBES-PEOPLE.

have been handed over to justice as a disturber of the peace. On the other hand, a large sum of money is at stake, and the Pathan does not "part." These little sidelights on the Pathan character are transparently visible in his choice of arguments. (I, must admit that I was unable to follow the arguments, conducted as they were in the Pushto tongue, but the dumb-show was eloquent to a degree.)

See that aged patriarch in the centre, with the flowing snow-white beard and the dignity of an Abraham. He has not said much yet, but sits in silence, shielding his eyes from the glare of the sun. The two old men on either side of him are doing all the talking, and from the tones of their voices it is easy to see with what cunning deftness they are putting their case before the Justice of the Peace. Resignation, aggrieved and pathetic; indignation, scornful and well simulated; wrathful outbursts and spasms of mock-humility, each in turn fail to move the Political Agent from his impartial summing-up of the case, in which character-study aids largely in sifting the truth from the untruth. Still the ancient patriarch opens not his mouth, and holds one with his quiet dignity. No doubt, as head malik of the tribe, he is too proud to sue for a slight reduction in the matter of the fine, and while his subordinates, from time to time casting a pebble on the ground in front of them by way of emphasizing a point, weave a voluble and circumstantial romance, if haply the fine may be eluded, he sits with studied indifference, making a little pattern with the pebbles at his feet.

But for all his air of dignity, he is not the noble patriarch you thought him. In a long life he has run the gamut of crime, from petty larceny to murder, and has seen the inside of Kohat Gaol more than once. Furthermore, his dignified silence is not the expression of a wounded pride, but an indication that, like a spoilt child, he is at this moment merely very sulky.

From Sadda Post to Parachinar the road runs parallel to the beetling range of the Sofaid Koh. None of the passes over this range into Afghanistan, which lies beyond, is under 12,000 feet high. The crest of the range is some 2,000 feet higher, rising at its western extremity to a height of 16,620 feet in the snowy peak of Sikaram. To the west of Sikaram lie the low hills of the Peiwar Kotal, the point of British territory nearest to Kabul, and beyond this, again, can be made out the elephant-shaped mountain in Afghanistan, over the brow of which runs the Shutargardan, or Camel's Neck Pass, and the road to Kabul. It was through here that Lord Roberts led his column into Afghanistan in 1879.

Parachinar is an open cantonment, and, owing to its altitude of 5,750 feet, would make an ideal hill-station. Here are the headquarters of the Kurram Militia and the political agency. The whole British staff, however, only amounts to eight men—viz., five officers of the militia, the Political Agent, a sapper, and a doctor. By these the whole of this valley, sixty miles in length and in area about the same size as Cambridgeshire, is administered.

The inhabitants of the Kurram are Turis. By religion they are Shias, and have, in consequence, always been at enmity with the surrounding tribes, who are Sunni Mahommedans, by whom they might well in time have been exterminated. But in 1893, at their request, the valley was occupied by the British, since when the Turis have been left more or less in peace by their neighbours. A small portion of the Bangash tribes in South-East Tirah profess the Shiah creed, and, like all other sects, are divided up into factions. These factions are led by different Saiyids (descendants of the Prophet), and are at constant enmity with one another. The Turi Saiyids are divided into two great factions, of which the Mian Murid, whose present leader, Mir Akbar Mir, resides in Tirah, though numerically inferior to the Drewandi, possesses by far the greater power of the two, owing to the lack of combination among the latter, and the jealousy which prevents the selection of a supreme head.

The Turis enjoy a reputation for bravery equal, if not superior, to that of any other Pathan tribe, else had they assuredly been exterminated long since. The raising of the Kurram Militia put them in a position to defend themselves against the Shinwari and Orakzai tribes to the north and the Khostwals to the south. As in the Khaibar, so here there are numerous posts along the road, and communication is kept up between these by means of heliograph, at which the native jemadars are adepts. Having learnt the Morse code and its equivalents in the English alphabet, they are enabled to speak to each other in their native language, Pushto, through this medium, even though in some cases they are unable to write their own language.

Khost is a small district of Afghanistan abutting directly on the southern boundary of the Kurram Valley, and jutting out wedgelike into the Bannu district. It commands the Bannu road to Miram Shah in the Tochi Valley, or Northern Waziristan. When we took over the Kurram and occupied the Tochi Valley in 1893-1895, the Amir Abdurrahman is said to have exclaimed: "These are two knives in my side!" With greater justice we might well reply that Khost has been a thorn in ours. Separated from its natural markets, Kohat and Bannu, the hostility of its inhabitants towards us has gradually increased, alternating, curiously, from time to time with intimations that they were ready to throw over the Amir if we would consent to take over their country. It has for long been a ready place of refuge for all the blacklegs of the border, offering as it does a secure retreat from which they might harry the Bannu border. Many a Hindu has been kidnapped and carried off into

Khost to be held to ransom by the outlaws. Efforts were from time to time made to procure the dispersal of these bands, but it would appear that the Hakim of Khost was in league with the outlaws, for the raiding never stopped for any length of time. Emboldened by the distractions that were occupying the attention of the authorities in other parts of the province all through last year, the raiding became more frequent than before. The crisis was reached in September, when a Jemadar Adjutant of the Northern Waziristan Militia, named Muzaffer Shah, together with several sepoys, was carried off from Datta Ismail Khel by a notorious outlaw named Arangi and his gang. Hitherto the Khostwals had been content to direct these personal attentions to Hindus, but the capture of a Government servant in the shape of a native officer of a frontier militia was a direct challenge to the Government of India. No ransom was forthcoming, but on November 7 news was received that the Jemadar had been released, after a captivity lasting two months. A declaration issued some days later by the Amir, to the effect that all outlaws were to be banished fifty miles from the Durand line, let drop a hint as to the means by which his liberation had been effected.

Between Thall and Bannu there is a wedge of independent territory jutting out into administered territory, and commanding the Kohat-Thall and Kohat-Bannu roads, through which the raiders from Khost were obliged to pass. While the recent kidnapping of Hindus from the roads was at its height, a cordon of troops was placed along a line indicated by Spinwam and Edak, for the purpose of intercepting the outlaws. Should the proclamation of the Amir fail to produce any effect, it will probably be found necessary to make this line a permanency.

CHAPTER VII

SOUTHERN WAZIRISTAN

THE development of the railway system in the North-West Frontier Province, considering its vital importance from strategical considerations, leaves a great deal to be desired. The value of such schemes as the Kurram Valley and Kabul River Railways lies chiefly in their more or less problematical utility at some future date, and their construction can only be justified by the supposition that at some future date that chain of circumstances will arise which will lead to the necessity of launching a large force into Afghanistan. But with regard to the administered districts of the province it is quite different. Many arguments, not least of which is the civilizing effect of railways, can be brought forward in support of their construction. At the present time there is no railway connecting Peshawar with the southern portions of the province. To reach Dera Ismail Khan, for instance, from Peshawar, it is necessary to undertake either a long and uncomfortable journey of some 200 miles by tonga via Kohat and Bannu, or an equally unpleasant railway journey by way of the Attock Bridge and the left bank of the Indus. Various schemes have from time to time been *sub judice* for linking up, not only the northern and southern parts of the province, but the whole province, with the Baluchistan Agency. Expense, however, has stood continually in the way of their realization. But the difficulty of rapidly transferring troops from Peshawar to the Derajat constitutes such a weakness in our system of frontier defence that the question of further railway construction is recognized in many quarters as being one of primary importance. Had the money that was spent on the abortive Kabul River Railway been expended on a line through the Kohat Pass to Kohat and Bannu, with a branch line from Bahadur Khel to Thall, a valuable and lasting work would have been effected, with, perhaps, less likelihood of stirring up the ill-feeling of the tribes than there was in the former case. From Bannu the line could then, in the course of time, have been continued via Laki and through the Pezu Pass, in the Khuttak country, to Dera Ismail Khan. From Pezu also, which is in the neighbourhood of Sheikh Budin, the hill-station of Southern Waziristan, a further extension could be made south-westward through Tank to the mouth of the Gumal. Its ultimate continuation through the Pass would depend on the state of the tribes in the Sherani country. A glance at the map will convince anyone of the undoubted strengthening in our military position that would result from such construction.

No doubt in time something of the sort will be done, but the midnight change at the miserable little junction of Kundian, and the bitterly cold drive on a winter's morning across the bed of the Indus from Darya Khan to Dera Ismail, is an experience that most people would not willingly undergo a second time. Dera Ismail is separated from Darya Khan in winter by twelve miles of sandy river-bed, with an occasional pontoon-bridge over the last remaining threads of the Indus, which meander along sluggishly towards the sea. In summer a swollen stream—not very deep, it is true—extends from bank to bank, and the river-ferries take sometimes as much as eight hours getting across. The reason of this is that the river is so encumbered with shifting sandbanks that the small steamers have now to steam upstream, and now to drop down a little with the current, so as to avoid them.

The track along which we drove across the Indus, changing horses twice, was marked out by a fence of rushes erected on the windward side of the road, so as to guard against its obliteration by drift-sand. Now and again we traversed tracts of low-lying sedge and rushes, known by the descriptive name of "jheels"—the haunt of bittern, snipe, and quail. From time to time a partridge scurried across the track in front of the galloping horses. Whenever a pontoon-bridge came into sight the tonga-wallah would blow a soul-stirring blast on his broken-winded bugle, to warn all and sundry whom it might concern that the mail was approaching, and that on no account should the slow-footed caravans venture on the bridge until it was safely past. The passage of a kafila several hundred yards long is an affair of at least a quarter of an hour.

The change in the scenery of Dera Ismail Khan from that of Peshawar is very striking. A new climatic belt has been entered. Here the date and other palms flourish in profusion, and brilliantly coloured parroquets flash in and out of their shade, uttering harsh and discordant cries. The bright sunshine, the whitewashed bungalows, and the luxuriant green of the vegetation, give the lie to its nickname of Dreary Dismal. But to live there is perhaps to understand. Dera Ismail is in constant danger of being engulfed by a sudden change in the course of the river, and the present site of the town dates only from about half a century ago. The new Paharpur Canal, which takes off from the Indus some 100 miles farther north at Balakot, passes close by here, and falls again into the Indus a little below. It was intended to irrigate the country round Paharpur lying to the north of Dera Ismail Khan, and to supersede the ancient and little scientific practice of damming up the torrent-beds till the water should back up above the level of the banks, and be led off at right angles over the fields. The advantage of the new canal lies in the fact that it renders *perennial* irrigation possible. The old method depended entirely on the rainfall, which might prove insufficient, or, on the other hand, if very heavy, was more than likely to rush down with such force from the hills as to sweep away in one night the huge dam which it had taken the communal labour of several villages six months to build. Utter famine would in such cases result, necessitating a remission of the revenue-tax. When it is remembered that the "rains" are all over and done with in about a fortnight, it will be seen how precarious is this method of irrigation. The new canal is not yet in thorough working order, and no decision has yet been arrived at as to what tribe shall be allotted the land which, through it, will eventually be brought under cultivation. The scheme is known as the Paharpur Canal Colony, but it is to be hoped that such land will only be granted to tribes dwelling in the administered portion of the province, since it would be as unjust as impolitic to grant it to any independent tribe when there are so many of our own subjects with better claims. While on the subject of irrigation I should like to mention here that the general character of the soil and the aspect of the country through which the Paharpur Canal flows bear a striking resemblance to large portions of Persian Mekran, notably the coastal belt, through which the route of the Mekran Field Force lay. Reference to this will be made in a subsequent chapter.

The town of Tank, situated forty miles to the

north-west of Dera Ismail Khan and nine from the independent border, is at once the terminus of the tonga service and the jumping-off place for the Mahsud country. It is also the hereditary possession of the ancient Nawabs of Tank, whose ashes lie mouldering in the ruined cemetery in the picturesque palm-garden of the Nawabs. The present Nawab is something of an eccentric, devoting his time and his money to the breeding of greyhounds, hawking and coursing being still a favourite pastime of the local chieftains in this part of the world. The Nawabs of Tank have always been bitter enemies with the tribes of the Waziri border, though they do not appear to have been very successful in "keeping their end up" against their neighbours, but rather to have been utterly at their mercy until the arrival of the British flag.

To the south of Tank, some forty miles distant, rises the famous "Throne of Solomon," the Takht-i-Suliman, with its twin peak, the Kaisar Ghar. West and north is a level plain, inhabited by Bhitannis, beyond which a dreary and barren country rises up gradually to the snowclad peak of Pir Gal, at least forty miles off, in the Derwesh Khel country. Twenty-two miles west of Tank lies the British outpost of Jandola, and between this and Pir Gal is the country of the Mahsuds, comprising in all some forty or fifty square miles.

The occasion which led me to undertake my first camel-ride, from Tank to Jandola, was the annual meeting of the Mahsud jirga, for receiving their allowances or paying up the balance of their fines, as the case might be. The Mahsud jirga is a byword among the tribes from Chitral to the Gumal for turbulence and "shaitani" (devilry). Our party consisted of the Resident in Waziristan, Mr. J. Donald, C.I.E.; Major Jacob, who had come from Quetta for the purpose of enlisting Mahsud recruits in the Indian army; and Major Dodd, Commandant of the Wano Militia and Political Agent in Southern Waziristan. The cavalcade was further augmented by our respective bearers and a couple of sowars (troopers). Thus escorted, we rode out across the plain towards the wall of mountains. As we approached these the stately head of Pir Gal sank gradually out of sight, and we were not to see it again until we stood on the ramparts of Jandola. The route led up the valley of the Zam River, and the stream had to be forded many times. As usual, the way was crowded with herds of small brown cattle and flocks of goats, being driven along by wild and unkempt-looking savages, whose loose cotton pantaloons were girded up about their loins because of the continual fording that had to be done. Southern Waziristan is noted on the frontier for its mutton, and grazing disputes are not uncommon between the Mahsuds and their neighbours. The Bhitannis especially are always looking for trouble of this kind by grazing their flocks on the land that by long usage has become the recognized ground of the Mahsuds, and though the former always come off worst, generally having their flocks driven off, yet they never seem to learn by experience that the Mahsud is best left alone. Another source of income to the inhabitants of Waziristan is derived from the magnificent forests of "edible" pine which clothe the slopes of Pir Gal and the surrounding mountains in the Derwesh Khel country. These forests are at present undergoing, for lack of more efficient methods, a system of "robber exploitation," by which at least a third of every tree is wasted. When cut down they are then roughly squared with an adze, until about half the tree is lying in chips on the ground. The balks of wood that remain are then laboriously floated down the Zam River in long booms of pairs of logs tied end to end, being dragged over the shallows until the plain is reached, when they are conveyed two at a time on camels into Tank, and there sold. If a British occupation of the Mahsud country ever becomes a *fait accompli*, a forest officer would be as desirable an addition to the administrative staff as he would be in the forests of Dir at the present moment.

The last approach to Jandola, when once the open amphitheatre of hills had been reached, in the middle of which the fort is situated, led past a little oasis of fields, kept eternally green by an irrigation ditch which led along the face of the hillside. Formerly the fort was under the charge of a single British officer, but the strain of this solitary life proved too great, and now two officers go up from Dera Ismail Khan for two months at a time.

Certainly it would be difficult to find a more depressing and dismal place for a two months' sojourn than Jandola. The fort itself is small, the rooms dark and ill-lit by narrow windows placed high above the floor, a very necessary precaution against being shot through the window by some fanatical "sniper." Officers are not allowed to go farther than three-quarters of a mile from the fort, and even then must have an escort. The walls of the mess-room were covered with the artistic efforts of the various people who from time to time had undergone a two months' incarceration within the fort. Regimental crests predominated, those of the 19th Punjabis, 47th Sikhs, and 40th Pathans, being conspicuous examples. The homely gramophone grinding out "The Merry Widow" served in a measure to distract the mind from thoughts of the "markhor" on the neighbouring mountains—so near and yet so far. To relieve the daily monotony of this existence, Major McPherson, 40th Pathans, in charge of the fort at the time of my visit, had introduced the game of rounders to the notice of his sepoys, who entered into the spirit of the game as much as we did on the afternoon of our arrival. Many of the Mahsuds who had assembled in the "hujra," some 200 yards from the fort, came over to watch the game. Among them was an aged faqir with a scarred and wrinkled face, to which a blind eye gave a peculiarly malignant and uncanny expression. He was dressed in the foulest rags and carried a heavy bludgeon, following us about with the most unpleasant persistence, and muttering hoarse maledictions against us. Hoping to be rid of him, we presented him with a couple of annas, which he cast back in our faces with every sign of contempt. He was then "moved on" by the sepoys.

It is hard to realize the change that comes over such a barren and hideous country as this as evening draws in. The ochre-coloured circle of hills, that all day has quivered in the heated atmosphere, at twilight takes on a softer hue, and the play of colour as the sun sinks behind the violet hills would have caused Turner, could he have seen it, to despise his best masterpieces. As the desert breeze springs up the opalescent light dies away, Pir Gal flashes a last pale signal from above Wano Post, and everything is swallowed up in umber. A bugle sounds the "Retreat" and then the "Alarm," and immediately the whole of the troops in the fort are at their quarters, as if an attack were impending. This is frequently done for practice, as the fort is in reality always in a state of half siege. Every night the barbed wire that surrounds the fort is religiously linked up in front of the large gateway, and the flares of straw, which are ignited by a torch slung down a wire from the ramparts, are seen to be in order.

The Mahsuds have always been, without exception, the most turbulent tribe on the frontier, and commit outrages from a sheer irresponsible "Schadenfreude," which no amount of fining has availed to mitigate. But for many years past they have been under the evil influence of the Mulla Powindah, a fanatical and unscrupulous mountebank, who has aspired to recognition by the Government of India as the leading malik of the Mahsuds.

This man is of the Shabi Khel section of the Mahsuds, and started life as a vagrant "talib-ul-ilm" (seeker after knowledge) in Landidah, an isolated village in the Bannu district. He was the instigator of the night attack on Wano Camp in 1894, when he remained unheroically in the rear, beating a drum, while his yelling accomplices rushed headlong in among the lines of the Waziristan Delimitation Escort. From this time dates his influence in Southern Waziristan. His position was still further strengthened in 1900, when in a weak moment he was accorded an interview with the Political Officer, by which action Government virtually recognized him as a chief of the Mahsuds. This was one of the greatest mistakes that could have been made, and it has taken years to undermine the position he gained in consequence of this meeting. Among other things, it precipitated the crisis which led to the establishment of the Mahsud blockade in 1900-01, and had its indirect effects in the murders of Captain Bowring in 1904 and of Colonel Harman and Captain Donaldson in 1905, in which there is little doubt that the mulla had a hand.

This winter the Mulla Powindah announced his intention to be present at the deliberations of the jirga in a manner which suggested that he expected the Political Officer to come out a mile on the road to meet him. He was coldly informed that he might come as an ordinary Mahsud if he liked, but that he would be accorded no status as a malik. Incensed at this slight to his dignity and blow to his prestige, he promptly sought to incite the Mahsuds to some act of violence, in the hope of breaking up the jirga. In this, however, he was unsuccessful, which may be taken as a good omen for the future, and as an indication of the gradual decline of his influence.

The usual delays had postponed the assembly of the whole of the jirga for several days, with the result that I was reluctantly compelled to return to Peshawar in the middle of the most interesting part, so as to be there for Christmas. However, on the first day, which was chiefly taken up with settling the afore-mentioned grazing disputes, the opportunity occurred of taking several good photographs. While on the way back to Tank by a different route from that by which we had come, in the pass not a mile away, had we known it, was a party of Mahsuds just returning from a raid on certain Bhitanni flocks pasturing in the plain. Two days later, at the final sitting of the jirga, a free fight nearly occurred between the Derwesh Khel Wazirs and the Mahsuds, owing to some trivial debt. The majority of the tribes-people could not have known the cause of the dispute, yet they showed themselves perfectly ready to join in the fray, and it was

RICE FIELDS, KURRAM VALLEY.

THE MAHSUD MALIKS.

by the merest chance that bloodshed was avoided, through the presence of mind of Major Dodd, the Political Officer, who threw up the rifle of a man who was about to fire. This man admitted that he had not the faintest notion what the quarrel was about, and was grateful for having escaped the sword of Damocles in the shape of a blood-feud for the rest of his life.

CHAPTER VIII

THE POLICY OF NON-INTERVENTION

WITH the formation of the North-West Frontier Province was also definitely adopted the policy of non-intervention, or "conciliatory policy," which had been laid down for the guidance of the Government of India two or three years before by the Secretary of State in a comprehensive despatch of January 28, 1898. The kernel of this despatch was admitted by Lord George Hamilton in a later communication to be a "limitation of your interference with the tribes so as to" (quoting the despatch) "avoid the extension of administrative control over independent tribal territory." This policy, of which the advantages had been previously fully recognized even by Sir Robert Sandeman, the "moving spirit" and very embodiment of the principle of the "forward policy," was in reality no new departure from the practice of former Indian statesmen, since it had been, with the exception of the taking over of the Kurram Valley in 1892-93, consistently followed in respect of the whole frontier to the north of the Gumal. The reasons for which the forward policy came to be adopted, with such admirable results, on that part of the frontier known as British Baluchistan were almost entirely unconnected with any immediate and pressing need of controlling the tribes on that border. It was the anxiety felt at the rapid advance of Russia in Central Asia towards the Oxus, and the strategical advantages which the possession of Quetta would confer on us in the event of a Russian war, that rendered imperative the subordination of mere expediency in local affairs to those larger questions which might turn the scale against us in a Russo-British world-struggle for the Asiatic continent. Had it not been for these insistent military reasons, Sir Robert Sandeman, as he admits in his memorandum of September 27, 1890, would have remained an advocate of the policy of non-intervention.

"As regards the extension of British control over the frontier tribes not subject to the Amir, I would urge that the policy of conciliatory intervention has been forced upon us. It is an absolute necessity that we should defend the Kabul, Ghazni, and Kandahar line in Afghanistan in case of war with Russia. Were this not the case I would be an advocate of masterly inactivity instead of conciliatory intervention, and I should consider it a mistake to make any attempt to include within our control the fringe of independent tribes which lie between ourselves and Afghanistan proper."

With the disappearance of the Russian peril the forward policy falls to the ground.

That the forward policy has never seriously been put into practice in the North-West Frontier Province shows how early it had been recognized by the military advisers of the Government of India that, with the advent of the Russians on the middle Oxus, the *point d'appui* of a foreign invasion had shifted from Peshawar to Quetta, from the Khaibar to the Bolan Pass, and from the plain of Kabul to the desert wastes to the north-west of Kandahar. With regard to a Russian advance, it is now almost universally recognized that the Herat-Kandahar route is the only thinkable line. In British Baluchistan we hold the key to the situation, with Karachi as a base, Peshawar as a right, and Gwadur or Pasni on the Mekran littoral as a convenient left. The railhead of the Sibi-Quetta line is now at New Chaman, that of the Russians at Kushkinsky Post or Kushk, slightly nearer to Herat than New Chaman is to Kandahar. As all the world knows, materials are held in readiness at both places for building a railway to Herat and to Kandahar. The Russians could probably accomplish this in a shorter time than ourselves. That is all. Armageddon would then be fought in the northern part of the Helmand Desert, which lies in between.

Although the pertinacious advocacy of the extension of the principles of the forward policy to the frontier north of the Gumal is an hereditary trait amounting almost to monomania among the frontier military, yet it will be seen that in the bsence of any special reason, such as that which led to the permanent occupation of British Baluchistan, the arguments adduced in its favour were not held to be sufficiently cogent to warrant its application on the Pathan frontier. Here the danger of arousing the active animosity of the tribes-people, possibly precipitating a general frontier rising, is thought to outweigh any strategical advantages that might accrue from such extension *vis-à-vis* the Russian question. The tranquillity of the frontier, in short, dominates all other considerations.

As evidence of this may be instanced the refusal of the Government in 1904 to comply with the request of certain Orakzai tribes of the Shiah faith, like the Turis of the Kurram Valley, on the southern confines of Tirah, to be taken under British protection, their land to be administered as British territory. This refusal was given in face of the recommendation of the military advisers of the Viceroy, who professed themselves ready, on its adoption, to withdraw the regular troops from the Samana Ridge, and to replace them with tribal militia. At the same time this recommendation was accompanied by another, in which it was urged that the time had come when we should gradually extend our "close control" up to the Durand line (Parliamentary Papers, N.W.F., Cd. 4201). The refusal of the Government was actuated by their disinclination to risk kindling the spark of disaffection among the Afridi tribes to the north, whose country would have been made—for them—unpleasantly accessible to British troops. Evidence of the feeling in Tirah against such a move was forthcoming in an unmistakable manner while the subject was still under discussion.

Instances where tribes have requested to be taken altogether under British control, in spite of their well-known love of independence, are by no means uncommon, and among these may be cited the Mahsuds, on all sides admitted to be the most independent and intractable tribe on the frontier.

At no time since the demarcation of the frontier by the Durand Mission in 1893 was so much care lavished on this portion of our Indian Empire as during the years of Lord Curzon's and Lord Minto's administrations. Not only were the frontier defences entirely reorganized, and the administration improved by the formation of the North-West Frontier Province, but this new policy, to which I have already alluded, was adopted towards the tribes. As an experiment this innovation was well worth the trial; as a *modus vivendi* it is as good as any that have been tried. And though it would be useless to claim for it that it has in any way provided the solution of the frontier problem, yet it would not be fair to attribute to it directly those regrettable incidents that have occurred since its inception. Many lessons and much valuable experience have been gained from it, which would not have been learnt in the school of the forward policy. It has served more than anything else to throw light on Afghan intrigue, and to show which way the wind is blowing in our buffer State.

During the whole of the period mentioned not a single square mile of territory was acquired, and in the only expedition of importance this principle was set forth in the most emphatic terms by the British Government, that "neither immediately or ultimately, directly or indirectly," should there be any idea of annexation; and though attempts were made to improve communications by the construction of here a metalled road, there a railway, these have been either necessary for the protection or convenience of our troops or complementary to our defensive alliance with the Amir, and their construction has in every case been subject to the consent of the tribes through whose territories they pass. Furthermore, owing to some inexplicable change of policy at the India Office, in two cases where strategical railways were in course of construction these have been abandoned. These were the Kurram Railway, in which work never proceeded farther than the acquisition of the right of way and the construction of the station bungalow at Parachinar, which is now its only memorial; and, secondly, the Loe Shilman or Kabul River Railway, on which work ceased some three years ago.

By these conciliatory methods it was designed, in the words of Mr. Chirol, to "win over the tribes by consent." The demarcation of the Durand line had left a bad taste in the mouths of the tribes on our side of the line. It was natural that they should fear that this was but the preliminary step to the occupation of their country—a feeling which the mullas were careful to stimulate with dark references to the fate of Egypt and the probable fate of Persia. It was thought that by calming these fears and by showing them that we had no designs on their territory beyond the exclusion of Afghan influences and the security of the persons and property of British subjects, we should gain the confidence of the tribes-people, and the raiding would eventually cease.

But the Pathan has always been an inveterate raider, and consistently hated and mistrusted us. Had we been able to exclude Afghan firebrands from Tirah, Waziristan, and the Mohmand country, success might have followed. For, in spite of the treachery, the cruelty, the avarice, and the cunning with which most writers have hitherto credited him, one cannot help feeling a pang of admiration for his high courage, often heroism, his powers of endurance, and his manliness—qualities which need but to be developed to make him into the splendid material of which the frontier militias can show such conspicuous examples. Here, one feels, is better stuff than the flabby down-countryman, with his timid effeminacy, and one who, could we but overcome this seemingly insuperable barrier of mistrust and misunderstanding, would not be insensible to the benefits of ordered government, nor turn and rend the hand that gave it. For in their dealings with us they have shown themselves not always oblivious to the higher dictates of honour; but in many things the Pathan is a spoilt child, and must be treated as such. It would be foolish to judge him by our own standards of right and wrong. Murder to him is not a crime, but a creed; robbery a social duty. He fails to grasp the theory of punishment, though admitting its practice with sulky resentment. Childish in his mental attitude towards our parental corrections, he is apt to be suspicious of our kindnesses, and to attribute wrong motives to any leniency shown him. Philanthropy is lost upon him. It does not enter into his conception of the social virtues. To him might is right, and any clemency is put down to the score of weakness. A policy of "masterly inactivity" leads him to the conclusion that we are incapable of taking his country from him, and one of concession that we dare not. As this opinion gains ground among the tribes-people, so the danger of a rising increases. And so the raiding continues, and the cry goes up that the "conciliatory policy" is a leaky vessel. Whenever the disturbances show signs of abating, a judicious prod with the Afghan stick is sufficient to stir the smouldering fires of fanaticism, and to cause little fires among the mountains, which, if neglected, threaten to spread and to cause a vast conflagration. And this is, in fact, what has been happening. There can hardly be any doubt that the activities of the fanatical Mulla Powindah among the Mahsuds, as well as the martial ardour of the Zakka Khel, and the rumours of conspiracy between the tribes north and south of the Kabul River, derive their motive force from Kabul. At the Mahsud jirga held at Jandola at the end of December, 1910, it was known that the Afghan Government had taken measures to keep themselves fully informed of its proceedings.

Disgusted by an apparently week-kneed policy of indecision, which forbids any firm grappling with the situation, and all unaware of the higher policy to which the local questions of the frontier must always be subordinated, it is hardly a matter for surprise that some voices are raised more and more as time goes on in favour of a reinitiation of the forward policy as the only solution of a very difficult problem.*

Looking at the question of moving up to the Durand line merely as a question of theoretical policy, and without regard to the situation at the present moment, both on the frontier and in India —in other words, to the fitness of the opportunity —there is much to be said on either side.

Viewed from the purely military standpoint, there can be no doubt as to the desirability of an advance. The only alternative involves a pusillanimous retreat, and the formation of a strong line of defences on what is known as the "inde-

* See note at end of chapter.

pendent border." Being at right angles to the Durand line, our present position violates one of the elementary rules of strategy. Should the internal condition of Afghanistan ever necessitate our intervention—a by no means hypothetical contingency—our only lines of advance are flanked on either side by presumably hostile tribes, demanding a force for the protection of communications altogether out of proportion to the actual fighting force employed. In the event of a border rising these isolated posts form a positive weakness, as they are easily cut off and have to be relieved. The siege of Chitral in 1896 and the burning of Landi Kotal in 1897 are cases in point.

It is evident that the Government realize the insecurity of these posts, since from time to time the question of evacuating the Wana Plain in Southern Waziristan is raised, and the retention of Chitral has already been condemned by expert military opinion. The cumbrous machinery by which we retain our hold on this remote stronghold is in itself a demonstration of the risks we run in this direction.

Opportunities, to be sure, have not been lacking had we intended to occupy the country. There is even reason to believe that a few of the tribes would secretly welcome our coming as a means to putting a stop to their blood-feuds, which in some cases have assumed such proportions as to threaten the extinction of whole clans, and that they would only make a small show of resistance, in order to "save their face" and to satisfy their own honour. As far back as 1880, when the Mahsuds sacked and burned Tank, at the supposed instigation of Shere Ali, the punitive expedition which followed in 1881 found the Mahsuds not inimical to a British occupation of their country.

But military opinion differs from political, and political opinion differs according as to whether its source is north or south of Tirah, which, running eastward as the country of the Jowaki Afridis to within fifteen miles of the Indus, cuts the North-West Frontier Province neatly into two. The nearer one approaches to the Baluchistan Agency in the south the more the methods of Sandeman find favour; but at the same time it is impossible to conceal the fact that the Khaibar is the pivot on which turns the frontier question, and that on *its* needs policy will be moulded and the event decided.

One of the most plausible arguments of the Baluch school is that the occupation of British Baluchistan has resulted in the complete pacification of that district. Deprecating the suggestion that the Baluch character is not so fiercely warlike as the Pathan, its votaries point out that north of the Sibi-Quetta line the Zhob Valley is, in point of fact, inhabited by Kakar Pathans. To clinch this argument the occupation of the Kurram Valley is cited. Where else in the province can one point to an open cantonment, as in Parachinar, only fifteen miles from the Afghan border, and fifty-seven from the nearest British fort—that of Thall, where even the dak-bungalow is situated for safety's sake within the walls?

It cannot be denied that, as a result of taking over the Kurram, the valley now presents, in the material prosperity and friendly character of its inhabitants, a marked contrast to its independent neighbours. But it must not be forgotten that the Turis owe us a debt of gratitude for having saved them as Shia Mahommedans, from extermination by their surrounding enemies of the Sunni persuasion—Shinwaris and Orakzais to the north, and Khostwals to the south—and that it was at their express invitation that we marched up the valley. Moreover, by so doing there was no chance of raising disaffection in Tirah through a mistrust of our ulterior motives on the part of the Afridis. As for any comparison that Baluchistan may be thought to afford with the North-West Frontier Province, the differences between the two in respect of distance from the Afghan capital and of population per square mile contribute to render unreliable any conclusions based on inference from one to the other.

On the score of expense, too, serious objections can be brought, not so much on account of actual military expenditure at the time, but because the revenue to be derived from a tract of country which, when not desert, is poor grazing land, would never support the army of revenue officials necessary for its collection. True, there are forests in Southern Waziristan which might produce considerable revenue, but these are chiefly owned by the Derwesh Khel Wazirs, a tribe to whom it appears we have virtually passed our word never to attempt to make them pay revenue. Thus the funds for running the administration would have to come out of the pocket of the already overburdened Indian taxpayer. Nor does irrigation hold out any prospect of converting independent territory into a "paying proposition," because, owing to the limited quantity of water available, for every new area put under irrigation, a similar area goes out of cultivation. It was calculated that if a scheme for irrigating 7,000 acres in Kurram—where taxes are nominal—were put into operation, a corresponding area in Bannu, which yields a considerable revenue, would be turned into a desert.

But there are even more pertinent objections to a forward movement being made, with which the perils of the moment are intimately connected. Were we to absorb independent territory, our administrative boundary would be conterminous with that of Afghanistan, and continual friction would ensue. Outrages committed by independent tribes can be punished according to British law or tribal custom without loss of prestige to Government; but such offences, when committed by Afghan subjects in British territory, constitute an act of aggression, and international issues are immediately thereby raised. The Amir would then no longer be able to shelter himself under the specious plea that he is no longer responsible for outrages perpetrated in independent territory. Any untoward incident in that case would spell Habibullah's downfall, for he would stand between the devil and the deep sea. On the one hand he must live up to the agreements which his father made with the British Government, and which is the price he pays for our support; on the other he must face his brother, with the whole weight of a fanatical hierarchy at his back.

In short, were we to occupy independent territory we should inevitably be drawn into a war with Afghanistan—a war of far-reaching consequences, and a responsibility against the assumption of which all the canons of common sense combine to militate.

For in the present condition of India sufficient troops could not be spared for such an enterprise, and it is doubtful whether reinforcements from home could be counted on. Furthermore, a war with Afghanistan would alienate the 70,000,000 Mahommedans in India, on whose support we can rely, at any rate for the present, owing to their rivalry with the Hindu population. Then there would be the question of holding Afghanistan, which would constitute a severe drain on the Indian exchequer and immobilize some 30,000 troops. For this service Pathan troops could obviously not be selected, and it would probably be found necessary to increase their pay considerably before Sikhs or Dogras could be got to serve there.

It is now barely three years ago that we were

saved, by the conclusion of peace with the Zakka Khel, from being involved in a combined rising of the tribes to the immediate north and south of the Khaibar, which, for reasons which need not be entered into here, would almost certainly have precipitated a war with Afghanistan. Practically the same thing occurred again in the autumn of last year, and this time the whole border from Chitral to the Takht-i-Suliman was looking to the Zakka Khel for a sign that was never given.

Whatever mistakes have been made in the past, it will be seen, with this knowledge to guide us, that our duty lies, not in "rattling the sabre," but in backing up the "man on the spot," whose efforts are at this moment directed towards staving off the explosion which all are agreed must come sooner or later, and, in the meanwhile as far as possible minimizing the effects of an evil, which it is impossible to root out, well knowing that in the hold we have over the trade-routes into India we wield a weapon less dangerous than "cold steel," but of proved efficiency.

NOTE.—*Vide* article in the *Globe* of October 15, 1910: ". . . The situation has now become intolerable, and the condition of the frontier to-day is a disgrace to any civilized nation which pretends to rule and give security in an alien country. What we have now to ask ourselves is whether it is not time for us to reconsider our frontier policy, and to advance our administration gradually up to the Durand Line. . . .

The reader may judge for himself what reliance may be placed in this exponent of frontier policy, who, a few lines farther down, refers to Dir and Upper Swat as among those districts that have already been taken over by the Administration.

CHAPTER IX

A CRUISE IN THE PERSIAN GULF

It had been my intention to return to England via the Persian Gulf and the Baghdad-Aleppo route, and with this object in view I sailed from Karachi on February 9 in the British India s.s. *Dwarka*, fast mail for Muscat, Bushire, and the head of the Gulf. Fate, however, decreed otherwise, and a month later I found myself once more in Karachi. Early on the morning of the second day out the high Arabian tableland which backs the Sultanate of Oman inland came faintly into view in the offing, and an hour or two later we steamed slowly into Muscat Harbour, past H.M.S. *Fox*, one of the cruisers engaged in the gun-running blockade. With the customary salute of three guns in honour of the Sultan, we came to anchor opposite the solitary gunboat which constitutes the Sultan's navy. An hour later, from the veranda of the British Consulate, I watched the *Dwarka* steam away for Bushire, while far away to the north a tiny panache of smoke on the sky-line, showed where the "slow mail" was labouring on her way to Jask, on the opposite Persian coast.

The little cove of Muscat, with its tiny town huddled together at the base of the cliffs, is a picturesque and compact little place. On either hand, overlooking the town, rise the twin castles—last remnant of Albuquerque and the Portuguese dominion—with their serried tiers of cannon pointing in every direction. Some of these, on a visit to the more easterly castle, called Fort Jellali, proved to have the five bezants of Portugal emblazoned on the barrel, while others had the monogram G.R., and are the remains of the armament of a British "74" presented to a former Sultan by the East India Company. The western castle is fast falling into ruins, and quite recently a large mass fell away from the wall of the central keep, which now presents a similar appearance to the "gesprengte Turm" of Heidelberg. The Constable of Fort Jellali is a Subadar in the Sultan's bodyguard. He was an aged man, and excused himself from accompanying me over the castle on the plea of asthma. I asked him if he would allow me to take his photograph, but this he also declined, on the ground that he was not in uniform. On the eastern face of the castle—that is to say, on the seaward side—the ground slopes away to a sally-port at the foot of the hill. From above a long line of whitish cliffs can be seen stretching away to the south-east, with never an inlet or bay, to the heights of Jabal Akhtar, in the dim distance. Far below, a dhow is beating up the coast in the teeth of a strong breeze, and in imagination it is easy to conjure up the scenes of bygone times, when Muscat was the home of piratical slave-traders and corsairs, sweeping the seas from Cape Mussendam to Ras-el-Hadd. For all that, the Portuguese castles give a curiously European air to the scene, as of the Western Mediterranean. One could imagine almost that the castle were inhabited by Knights Templar, and that the pirates were the Moorish corsairs of the African main.

At the back of the town rise barren and pointed peaks of no great height, quivering in the heat, and each surmounted by a watch-tower. These watch-towers are found to be needful in case of any sudden attack by the nomad Bedouins of the interior, an occurrence by no means infrequent in former years. At night-time the watchmen in these towers keep up an incessant chant in a minor key, calling from one to the other a mournful refrain, which produces a curiously melancholy effect when heard for the first time. It is this mournful chant and the still tropic night of Muscat that constitutes the individual charm of the place, and it is that which comes into my mind as I look back to the week I spent there.

The streets and bazaars of Muscat are narrow and dirty to a degree, and peopled with the most hideous specimens of humanity that I have ever seen. Ordinarily the men are wiry and of an unmistakable Arab strain, but the women—at least, those that are to be seen in the streets—are of negro or Suaheli origin, with flat noses, thick lips, and an oily and repulsive appearance. Whether from personal vanity or from sheer compassion towards the unwilling spectator, they wear a black mask or visor, which still further contributes to their terrifying ugliness. The inhabitants live chiefly on fish and dates, a large quantity of which is imported from the opposite coast of Mekran. Tunny are caught and offered for sale on the beach, where by midday may be seen a festering heap of ichthyological remains, sweltering under a swarm of flies.

The town itself is surrounded by walls, there being two gates on the landward side: the Little Gate, which leads nowhere in particular, and the Great Gate, which leads through a pass to the neighbouring village of Mattarah, about three miles up the coast. Mattarah is the commercial quarter of Muscat, and from thence all the caravans start for the interior of Arabia. Muscat is unapproachable from inland except by this route. To gain the town from the side on which the British Consulate is situated, it is necessary to pass through a gate over which is still a banner with the word "WELCOME" in large letters, which was put up on the occasion of Lord Curzon's visit to the Gulf in 1903. These three gates of the city are always locked at night, for fear of a Bedouin raid.

As the centre of the arms traffic in the Gulf, Muscat naturally bristles with rifle depots and stores. The Custom House quay is seldom unencumbered with cases of rifles and ammunition, while every other shop in the bazaar is a rifle-shop

MUSCAT.

LANDING AT BAHREIN.

There is a certain amount of humour in a situation in which a British cruiser is actually at anchor in the harbour, with a dhow loaded to the water-line with rifles and ammunition almost within a cable's length of her, a Custom House quay fairly crowded with large wooden crates containing the same, and a bazaar simply bursting with arms and ammunition. But the laugh is on our side, and I am credibly informed that, owing to the thoroughness displayed by the blockading squadron, there are now in Muscat itself at least 200.000 rifles and probably 3,000,000 rounds of ammunition for which a market cannot be found. Prowling through the town one day, I entered a house, and was shown upstairs by an obsequious chuprassi to an upper room, where an Arab was sitting at a roll-top writing-desk, directing the operations of two servants, who were packing up box after box of Indian rupees, ready for being despatched to Karachi. I appeared to have chosen a busy time for my visit, but made myself known as an English traveller wishing to see as much of Muscat as I could. I learnt that my interlocutor was Ali Musa, the agent for Messieurs Goguyer Frères, the principal arms-traders in Muscat. Ali Musa is an Algerian, and we conversed in French. He told me that *les affaires* were not progressing as satisfactorily as *dans le temps*, owing to the watchfulness of the blockading squadron. He hinted, however, that the trade was not yet at an entire standstill by any means, and that secret channels of egress existed, which were being developed, and which would prove troublesome to us in the future. After this he became more reticent, and I took my leave. On the whole there is little hostility to Englishmen in Muscat, whose inhabitants take a sportsmanlike zest in outwitting us if they can, taking defeat with good grace and a smile, which tells that they do not consider themselves to have had altogether the worst of the game. A friend of mine told me that one day he went into the bazaar to buy a rifle, but that the vendor refused to sell him one, saying, "If you want rifle, you go and get him out of sea." This, of course, had reference to our practice of "dumping" captured rifles overboard.

To the courtesy of Major Trevor, the British Chargé d'Affaires in Muscat, to whom I also owe a debt of gratitude for his kind hospitality to me, I owe it that I was received by the Sultan, and, though it was impossible to touch on any subject however remotely approaching political questions, or those connected with gun-running, yet sufficient was said to convince me that a very real value is placed on the continuance of friendly relations between Muscat and the Government of India. The Sultan received us at the door of his palace, and led us upstairs to a room on the first floor, overlooking the harbour. On a black-and-white marble floor, in the middle of the room, was an oak table, on which stood a globe of the world, to which he frequently referred in the course of our conversation. Round the table were a few chairs, and a divan ran the length of one wall, which was decorated with steamship notices of the North German Lloyd and other lines. On a shelf stood two enormous "beaked" coffee-pots, of the kind usual in the Gulf. Presently the Sultan rose and conducted us into an adjoining room, and proceeded to put on an embroidered robe of State, which I gathered he had worn at the time of Lord Curzon's visit a few years before. This apartment was furnished in a more Oriental style than the first, the walls being decorated with mirrors and coloured glass. On the table was an emu's or ostrich's egg, several shells, and numerous European novelties and knick-knacks, and in one corner was a telephone, connecting the palace with two Portuguese forts. The Sultan is a middle-aged man, inclining to stoutness, with a manner in which dignity and bonhomie contend for the mastery. The following day I happened to meet him again in the bazaar, taking a morning stroll with his Court. He was dressed in a Norfolk jacket and wide, baggy trousers, and wore a turban. He had just been inspecting his stable, which consisted of a number of well-bred Persian horses picketed in an open space in the town. As there is no possibility of riding, or even exercising, them in Muscat, it is difficult to see for what reason they are kept, unless it be that in every Arab there is implanted the love of horse-flesh.

The little European community that is condemned to pass a few years in Muscat consists of a French, an Italian, an American, and a British Consul—there is not yet a German Consulate—a British telegraph-master, a British doctor, and the agents of one or two trading firms. Lawn-tennis is the only form of recreation which it is possible to obtain, and the little colony meets in the evening for a set or two, to which the cruisers in the harbour contribute sometimes a welcome addition in players. Lunching one day on board the *Fox*, Captain Hunt showed me afterwards an ingenious invention which he had contrived for fishing at sea while under steam. It was an automatic device for taking up the strain on the line when a fish was caught, and obviated the necessity of keeping a constant watch on the line. By a system of weights attached to the line, which had been rove through a block at the masthead, a fish of, say, twenty-five pounds would raise a shot of approximately the same weight, with a rush halfway to the truck, and would be brought up gradually by the second weight attached farther down the line coming into play. Should a fish of 100 or even 150 pounds weight be hooked, the weight would be thus automatically increased, as the successive shot were raised from the ground, until a sufficient drag had been produced. The strain caused by hooking a large fish while steaming at ten knots would otherwise probably snap the line. With a large spinning-bait tunny of 50 or 60 pounds had been caught, but the possibility of catching a shark had necessitated the employment of shot of an aggregate weight of 250 pounds.

The phosphorescent effect produced at night by the presence of the red Sargasso weed* in the harbour of Muscat was sometimes very beautiful, and the light was occasionally so strong as to throw a glow over Fort Jellali up to the very battlements. The weed appeared to drift in from the open sea when the wind set from the Indian Ocean.

Having spent just a week in Muscat, I sailed on a Monday in the slow-mail for Jask, where we stayed long enough to permit of my lunching on shore with Colonel Whyte and the officers of the detachment of the 117th Mahrattas, who are stationed there for the protection of the Indo-European telegraph-line and the new "wireless" installation, by which the cruiser squadron are kept informed of the movements of suspicious dhows. Landing at Jask, as at all other points along this narrow and shelving shore, is rendered difficult by the dangerous surf, which beats constantly on the beach even in the calmest weather. It is necessary to anchor some distance offshore, and then back down the boat astern till near enough in to jump ashore. The steamer, of course, cannot come within two miles of the shore, but anchors in Jask

* I am not aware of the proper scientific name of this plant, though the reader, if he wish, could decide for himself approximately by consulting the list of seaweeds found on the island of Henjam, given at the end of Floyer's "Unexplored Baluchistan."

East or West Bay according to the direction of the wind.

The importance of Jask lies in the fact that it is the point where the threads of three cables, one overland telegraph, a local telephone system for the telegraph-huts, and the invisible threads of the "wireless," are gathered together in the hand of a superintendent, who is also the Political Officer.

At the time of my visit Jask presented the appearance of a miniature Ladysmith. On every hand sand-bag forts, surrounded with an inextricable network of wire entanglements, met the eye. Sand-bag forts also blocked the entrance to the main building, and more barbed wire. The whole cantonment was surrounded by a veritable zareba of barbed wire, from the middle of which two flagstaffs rose to the height of 150 feet from the ground. On the top of these more wire. From the neighbouring building an intermittent tearing noise indicated that the "wireless" was working. It was as if some gigantic bumble-bee had been caught in a labyrinthine spider's web, and was making efforts to escape. And this all because some 900 Afghans were on their way down from the north to bend the Baluch Sardars and the Arab "nakhudas" (skippers) to their will.

From the top of the telegraph building Old Jask is visible, the residence of the hereditary Mirs of Jask, and behind this, again, the arid coast range. The present Mirs of Jask, Mir Mustapha and Mir

Hoti, have gone down a bit in the world, and their more powerful neighbour, Mir Haji of Sakui (of whom more anon), wiped out Old Jask some years since. In summer the continually drifting sand raises a curtain in front of the coast range, so that nothing can be seen farther than a mile from Jask, and for all one can see, Jask might be situated in the middle of a vast plain as flat as a billiard-table.

We weighed anchor towards evening, with an addition to the cargo of several drums of barbed wire, so as to enable the Consulate at Bandar Abbas to put itself into a better position for defence against the expected onslaught of the Afghans.

While still on the subject of radio-telegraphy, it is an interesting fact that with a daylight radius of 300 miles it is impossible to communicate between Lingah and Muscat, though at night Bombay may sometimes be called up from Lingah, a distance about three times as great. It is said that one night Bombay refused to speak with Lingah, because they were "talking with the West Coast of Ireland." Whether there is some formation in the rocky promontory of Cape Massendam which interrupts the current is not known, but the wireless operator on the P. and O. *Salsette* told me he "could generally" speak to ships at the head of the Persian Gulf from the entrance to the Gulf of Aden—that is to say, across the whole extent of the Arabian plateau, a distance of over a thousand miles. This is, of course, only possible at night-time.

It was impossible to land either at Bandar Abbas or Dibai, the two next ports of call, and all the impression of them I retain is of a faint ribbon of palm-trees some four miles away, and an invisible line of sandy beach. Close to Bandar Abbas are the islands of Qishm, Henjam, Larak, and Hormuz, the last of which gives its name to the straits in which it is situated. On the eastern end of Larak are the remains of yet another Portuguese castle. At the western extremity of Qishm is the shallow harbour of Basidu, which has been used as a coaling station for the sloops and pinnaces of the blockading squadron. It is, however, too shallow to admit of the larger cruisers coaling there in comfort, and since the rest of the island belongs to Persia, there seems to be a general consensus of opinion that it would benefit all parties concerned were we to give up the harbour of Basidu in exchange for the small island of Henjam.

Dibai is situated on what is known as the "pirate coast," and is ruled over by one of the seven "trucial" chiefs, so called from the fact that after the suppression of the slave-trade they entered into treaty engagements with the British Government. The remaining trucial chiefs are those of Abu Thabee, Shargah, Ajman, Umm-al-Gawain and Ras-al-Kheyma. It was at Dibai that a landing-party from the *Hyacinth* was fired on on Christmas Day, while searching for concealed arms.

This led to the bombardment of the town, and the punishment of its chief. It is thought that the trouble began through the employment of a strategy of the natives, by which, under plea of removing their women-folk before the search, the arms were also removed at the same time, a trick which had succeeded more than once before.

The majority of the passengers on board were pearl-merchants returning from India, where they had been to dispose of their yearly output. The next port being Bahrein, and their destination, we were looking forward to being able to walk about the decks once more in comfort. I think we were justified in feeling a certain pleasure at their departure, since there were only about three of them who owned first-class tickets, the rest being slaves and acquaintances, who battened on the hospitality of the pearl magnates, and spread their carpets under our very feet as we walked the decks. Remonstrance with the captain was in vain. We were told that it was the company's orders that the Arabian passengers should be shown every consideration. And this they were, even at the expense of European travellers. We could only be thankful that we were not on board the same steamer on her way down the Gulf a few weeks later, when every flat surface that could be termed a deck would be crowded out with Arab horses and Arab horse-dealers.

The value of the pearl-trade of the Bahrein Islands appears to be steadily on the increase, and there seems to be an opening for some enterprising British firm to send an agent there annually. The figures, which are to be found in the Consular Report for 1910, are as follows:

1907–08	...	...	...	...	£285,400
1908–09	...	...	...	...	£140,000
1909–10	...	...	...	...	£420,667

The drop noticeable in the figures for 1908-09 is no doubt due to the financial crisis of that year in America, which reacted on both the American and British markets.

About seven miles inland from Bahrein are the ruins of an ancient civilization, thought at one time to be of Phœnician origin. It was even suggested by some that this place might be the cradle of the Phœnician race. Having the whole day in front of us, we determined to land and ride out on donkeys to this burial-ground. Our donkey-ride began sooner than we had expected, for the beach shelves down so gradually that it is impossible to get a boat within 50 yards of the shore, and after bumping over hard sand for a little way, we rode ashore on donkeys. With good trotting donkeys we did not take long to reach our destination. The track led through mile after mile of shady date-groves, till at last we came to the open salt-plain. Continuing some time over this, we came to another village, over which we could see the rounded tops of innumerable tumuli or barrows. Those nearest the village appeared to be larger than the rest; but there must have been several thousand of them, for they stretched away to the horizon, and, going back by another way, we came upon another field of them. A few of them were excavated some years ago by Professor Theodore Bent, but so little was found in them that it was not thought worth while continuing the excavations. Inside the mounds are large burial-chambers, some of them extending to a considerable depth underground, and constructed of enormous blocks of white limestone, roughly hewn and fitted together, forming what I believe is termed "cyclopean architecture." Dr. Budge is of opinion that they belong to a civilization vastly anterior to that of the Phœnicians, or, indeed, even to the Summerian or Accadian Empires of the Euphrates Valley. "And God planted a garden eastward in Eden. . . ." "Es lässt tief blicken."

From Bahrein we made for Bushire, and had again to undergo the discomfort of landing from the steamer at a distance of four miles from the shore. It is impossible for the British-India boats to enter the harbour of Bushire without touching ground, and since this is imperative to enter the Shatt-al-Arab, it is thought advisable to do so as little as need be at other places of call. A snapped propeller is not an easy thing to replace in the Persian Gulf, not to mention the cost of a bronze blade, which runs into hundreds of pounds. It is generally agreed that the situation of Bushire is such as to destroy any hope of it ever growing much beyond its present importance. The Karun on the one hand and Bandar Abbas on the other are two competitors whose rapid expansion will in the long run stifle the trade through Bushire. Its situation on an island, and the extensive dredging that would be necessary to convert its harbour into a safe anchorage for large steamers, are the two largest disadvantages against which it has to contend. The eventual tranquillity of the Southern Persian trade-routes is only a matter of time, but the trade of Ispahan will find a better outlet through the Valley of the Karun, that of Yezd through Bandar Abbas. There remains, therefore, but the trade of Shiraz.

At the time of my visit to Bushire, the Shiraz road was considered to be so unsafe that permission was refused to travellers wishing to proceed into Persia by that route. I remembered having read of the British "note" to Persia on this subject in the Reuter's telegrams at Port Said on my way out in October, and the incredulous surprise with which the news was received. The "note" still formed a chief topic of conversation, and it was laughingly said that an enterprising traveller, whose life was to him of no particular importance, might easily earn the lasting gratitude of his country by becoming the sacrificial calf, over whose dead body British troops might justifiably march to Shiraz to restore the tranquillity of the road.

The European Consulates at Bushire are for the most part situated at such a distance from the town that it is hardly a matter of surprise that in times of disturbance it becomes necessary to land troops from war-ships for their protection. In the centre of the town is the palace of the Darya Begi, or Governor of the Gulf ports, and in the harbour lies the *Persepolis*, the one battle-ship of the Persian navy. About three miles along the coast to the eastward are the Russian and German Consulates. Behind these, a little way inland, at Sabsabad, is the bungalow of the British Resident in the Persian Gulf, Colonel Cox. Yet farther inland, and equally isolated, are the bungalows of the Medical Inspecting Officer for the Gulf, and of Mr. Consul Chick and Mr. Birdwood, whose hospitality I had the honour of enjoying for two days.

Had I continued my journey in the "slow mail," I should have had an opportunity of visiting the harbour of Koweyt, about which, until recently, as the "only possible" terminus to the Baghdad Railway, there has been so much discussion. This theory has, however, been recently exploded, since it is now generally recognized that the dredging of the bar at the mouth of the Shatt-al-Arab is within the bounds of practical engineering. It is said that were Koweyt to be made the terminus of the Baghdad Railway, it would still pay the steamship companies to load up half bulk in Basra and the rest in lighters outside the bar, as is done at present.

Proceeding again from Bushire in the "fast mail," we passed the Turkish fort of Fao, at the mouth of the Shatt-al-Arab, at the same time bumping over the bar, and steamed up the Shatt-al-Arab, between wide banks covered with date-groves. These groves are among the richest in South-Western Asia, and extend for a mile or two on either bank. Behind them the land becomes low and marshy, and behind this, again, is the illimitable desert. On the right bank as we steamed up to Mohammerah floated a mirage, as of mist rising from off a lake. As far as Mohammerah and the mouth of the Karun, which here debouches at right angles into the Shatt-al-Arab, the eastern bank is Persian territory. From Mohammerah we went forward in Messrs. Lynch's launch to Basra, preceding the steamer by a day. It is not an uncommon thing for the launch to be fired on on its way up to Baghdad, and, though we saw the dents in her funnel and sides, we were fortunate in escaping the attentions of any riparian marksman.

From the Shatt-al-Arab branch off many canals at right angles, and on one of these, at about a mile from the river, is situated the native town, with its tortuous bazaars. Along its banks are the dwellings of the richer inhabitants and the few Europeans whose business necessitates their presence in Basra. On the river itself are the docks, wharfs, and quays of the shipping and trading firms. The appearance of this canal is picturesque in the extreme, and might be termed an Oriental Venice without prejudice to the latter. Up and down this waterway with amazing swiftness ply the long narrow native craft, propelled at each end by a picturesque savage, hardly less willowy in form than the punt-pole

THE GRAND CANAL, BASRA.

THE BRIDGE OF SIGHS, BASRA.

To face page 138.

which he so deftly wields. Halfway towards the native town is a wooden bridge, constructed of balks of timber lashed together. When I first beheld it, a small cavalcade of Bedouin cavalry was slowly making its way across it, their dirty garments contrasting ill with the Saracenic grace of their horsemanship. The yellow house behind, with its brilliant cobalt blinds, cast warm zigzaggy shadows in the water below.

Basra now boasts an hotel owned by a Greek, and at this we put up. With its untidy and scrupulously dirty "patio," it was not unlike a Spanish "posada" of the meaner sort. It was in no sense a pleasure to stay there, and we were glad we had some tinned Bologna sausage to fall back upon. Our spirits were, however, kept up by a party of three French engineers on their way to Aleppo. The doyen of this trio was accompanied by his wife, a charming lady. She, on hearing of the horrors of existence in Baghdad, declared with simulated horror that nothing would induce her to go a step farther. Her husband had surely mistaken his vocation, for in a deep base voice, evidently trained, he sung snatches from the opera with a wonderful pathos of expression. When he switched off into a less serious vein, his companions joined in with melodious tenor and alto.

The bazaars of Basra, though more extensive than those of any Gulf port I had yet seen, did not present any particularly new feature. The town is occupied by a Turkish garrison, and it would be difficult to imagine a tougher or more truculent-looking set of soldiers than these. It was with some little surprise that, on passing a group of three or four soldiers, I heard the familiar greeting "May you never be tired!" uttered in the Pushto tongue. A rather laboured conversation elicited the fact that these were Afghan and Pathan sepoys who had enlisted in the Turkish army. I cannot now remember from which part of the frontier the latter hailed, but I rather think it was from the Yusufzai side. The Afghans were Kabulis, and, since the Afghan army is trained by Turkish instructors, there is nothing so very remarkable in the presence of these Afghans in the Turkish army.

Instead, now, of continuing my journey to Baghdad, the possibility of an expedition being despatched to Mekran led me to retrace my steps to Karachi. Nothing of importance occurred on the return run, and the voyage, which had taken three weeks up the Gulf, was now accomplished in five days. However, on arrival in Karachi it appeared that there was no likelihood of such an expedition being sanctioned in the immediate future, and, since I was not due in Bombay till March 24, I set off to visit Lahore, Delhi, and Agra, with an account of which I do not intend to bore the reader.

CHAPTER X

GUN-RUNNING IN THE PERSIAN GULF

HITHERTO I had only had an opportunity of observing the effect of the gun-running on the Pathan tribes of the North-West Frontier. But during my cruise in the Persian Gulf, of which in the last chapter I gave a short narrative, I was enabled to learn considerably more of this interesting subject.

About the middle of February it began to be rumoured in various quarters that a large body of Afghans, numbering, it was said, 3,500, had been concentrating for some time past in the neighbourhood of Bampur, a town in Persian Baluchistan. The presence of Afghans in Persian Baluchistan was not in itself remarkable, since it is in spring that the Ghilzai traders visit the Gulf, on their way back from India through Afghanistan to Central Asia. But the gravity of the situation was to be found in the temper of the invaders, and, according to rumours that were current, their intentions were of the most warlike nature. They were reported to be contemplating a repetition of the outrage on the Central Persian Telegraph-Line of September, 1910, when four miles of wire had been cut up. An attack, under the leadership of Mir Barkat Khan, late Governor of Biyaban, on one or other of the small posts that have been established for the protection of the Indo-European Company's line at such places as Chahbar, Jask or Bandar Abbas, was also feared. Mulla Khair Mohammed of Karkindar in Karwan, commonly known as the "Khalifa Sahib," was also stated to be advancing at the head of a following of upwards of 200, accompanied by a wandering derwesh of "mystic powers."

Among the Afghan tribes none have benefited more by the arms trade, nor enjoyed greater facilities for embarking in this traffic, than the Ghilzais. These, besides being themselves the purchasers of large quantities of rifles, have gradually acquired almost a monopoly of the carrying trade in arms. Owing to the hostility of the Persians of Kerman, to the vigilance of H.B.M. Consul-General in Meshed, and, more recently, to the presence of a Gurkha regiment in Robat, the routes followed by the arms-caravan have of necessity been gradually narrowed down to an area indicated by an isosceles triangle, of which the apex is roughly at the Helmand Lake, and its base between Lingah on the west and Chahbar on the east. From the apex of this triangle the caravans cross the Afghan frontier to Bandar-i-Kamal Khan, on the Helmand River, thence along its banks to

Girishk, whence they branch off to Kandahar and Ghazni, the country of the Ghilzais.

This powerful and warlike tribe, the backbone of the Afghan nation, and our old enemies at Maiwand, is divided into two sections, of which the nomadic "Powindahs," or warrior-merchants, constitute the wealthier of the two. As traders between Hindustan and Khorasan (Herat, Bokhara, etc.), they are accustomed to fight their way through their hereditary enemies of the Mahsud and Waziri borders. They visit India during the cold weather to barter the merchandise that they have brought from Central Asia, leaving their families and their herds of camels in vast encampments on the banks of the Indus. It is estimated that 50,000 of them pass yearly through Dera Ismail Khan. They command a considerable credit among the Hindu bannias of Peshawar, Lahore, Delhi, and even Calcutta and Bombay. When the rapid development of the arms trade opened up an additional and more profitable field for trading, the Ghilzai merchants were not slow to seize the opportunity, and for some years now have had commercial relations with the principal arms-dealers of Muscat.

But it is to the second and more stay-at-home section of the Ghilzais, known as "Jais," or settlers, that the Afghans who had invaded Persian territory belonged. Though by no means so wealthy as the Powindahs, they, too, had invested large sums of money in the arms trade. The Sultan of Muscat, however, discouraged these

Ghilzai traders from coming in person to Muscat, fearing that it would prove prejudicial to his relations with the British Government, through whose instrumentality alone the Beduin tribes of the Omani hinterland are kept at bay. But in spite of this restriction, such was the confidence of the Ghilzais in the Muscat dealers that they continued to pay their money down, in the full certainty that the rifles would be duly delivered on the Mekran coast. The Muscat dealers undertook, in fact, to engage the dhows and make all arrangements for running the guns over to the Persian side, where, in their turn, the Baluch Sirdars found camels and acted as intelligence agents in the interests of the Ghilzais. The arrival of cargoes of rifles, watched for and marked by the Baluch Sirdars, was duly notified to the Afghans, who, owing to the lack of forage for their beasts near the coast, as well as to the need for secrecy, were expectantly waiting some ten or fifteen miles inland. When the coast was clear, they came down, loaded up the rifles, and the long march inland commenced, each successive chief through whose territory the caravan passed taking his toll.

Among the Baluch Sirdars of Persian Mekran the most indefatigable in the interests of the gun-runners has been Mir Barkat Khan, Governor of Biyaban up till the time of his capture in March, 1910—a man of more spirit than the majority of his race, and one who has presumably reaped a substantial harvest from his enterprise. So great, indeed, at one time was his activity as to cause the Persian Government anxiety as to the preservation of their authority in this district. He was in consequence one day spirited away on board the Persian cruiser *Persepolis* by the Derya Begi, or Governor of the Province of the Gulf Ports, who had been sent by the Persian Government for this express purpose.

Last August, however, he managed to effect his escape, and returned to Biyaban at an opportune moment for those engaged in the traffic, for the disorganization caused in the plans of the gunrunners by the vigilance of British cruisers in the Gulf of Oman had brought the trade to a standstill. Not only had dhows which had left Muscat been compelled, after a severe chasing, to put back to their port of departure to evade capture, but the "nakhudas," or Arab skippers, owing to the increased risk, refused any longer to run guns across on the same terms as before. The arrangement hitherto adopted had been the payment of a third of the value of the dhow to her owner by the Afghan trader, with an undertaking to pay up the remainder in the event of the ship being captured or otherwise lost. The nakhudas now demanded payment in full, as dhows were becoming scarcer and scarcer every day. In this condition the Afghans were unwilling to acquiesce, having no guarantee of the good faith of the nakhuda. Even Barkat Khan, with all his influence, proved unable to induce them to resume their occupation, and was also in consequence himself a loser.

The naval measures that resulted in this state of affairs are briefly as follows: The Omani and pirate coasts of Arabia are watched by cruisers, and the departure of dhows is communicated immediately on receipt of the intelligence by wireless telegraphy to Jask, whence the information is passed on to "boat-cruisers" that are stationed along the coasts of Mekran and Biyaban at the most likely landing-places. These boats contain an officer and from six to a dozen bluejackets, and are visited fortnightly by the cruisers to which they belong. Their occupants are frequently sniped from the shore, and when a strong "shumal" (north-west wind) is blowing, the only alternative to riding out the gale in very uncomfortable quarters is the hazardous venture of landing up a creek and accepting the risk of being fired on. Cruisers search dhows in Persian waters, in accordance with an agreement entered into with the Persian Government, but not in Muscat territorial waters, since it is suspected that the captured rifles, when returned to the Sultan, find their way back into the possession of the dealers. Precautions have also to be taken against any gun-running dhow getting through from Hodeidah or other Red Sea port. Information is generally available as to the presence and whereabouts of any large number of camels in the interior, which very often furnishes a clue to the place selected by the nakhuda for running the cargo. It is, however, not improbable that camels are collected in one place as a blind, while the rifles are being landed at another point.

Whether the continuance of the blockade will eventually have the effect of killing the trade altogether is a point on which it is difficult to form any opinion. Myself I do not think it will, and short of some definite arrangement with the French Government and with the Sultan of Muscat, by which the abrogation may be effected of the treaties which give to certain subjects of the Sultan the right to fly the French flag, and to the French and other nations the right of free trade with the port of Muscat, the presence of a cruiser squadron in the Gulf will remain necessary to check the traffic. For so long as these treaty rights enable the Sultan, without forfeiting the support that we afford him in his dealings with the Beduin tribes of the interior, to permit a trade which he knows to be contrary to our interests, but from which he is reported to levy a large sum in import duties, so long will he be in the enviable position of being able to "eat his cake and still keep it." Rumours have been afoot of proposals from the French Government for the relinquishment of these rights in return for the cession of a certain British possession in West Africa. Such a sacrifice, however, would hardly seem "worth the candle," and as things stand at present our only lever with the Sultan is his fear of a second sack of Muscat by Beduin invaders.

The traffic, nevertheless, has been greatly reduced. The constant harassing to which dhows have recently been subjected has undoubtedly caused many of the dealers in Muscat to transfer their business to other quarters, or to shut up shop altogether, owing to actual or imminent bankruptcy. Muscat is, of course, very closely watched, and quite recently in the harbour was to be seen a dhow, with 2,000 rifles on board, that had twice essayed without success to run through the tightly drawn cordon. This has led to an attempt to form depots farther up the coast. By this the additional advantage would be gained of being able to put straight across the Gulf of Oman at its narrowest part, instead of having to work laboriously up the coast (by night, so as to benefit by the off-shore breeze) before getting a fair wind. Depots were also probably formed on the pirate coast within the Persian Gulf. No doubt Dibai was one of these, though the punishment that was meted out to its sheikh will probably deter the remaining trucial chiefs from emulating his example. At present suspicion centres on Sohar, a port about a hundred miles north of Muscat, as a possible depot, the rifles being conveyed secretly from Muscat.

On the refusal of the nakhudas to continue operations as before, the Ghilzais demanded that the money they had on deposit in Muscat, as security for the guns they had caused to be ordered, should be refunded to them. This the dealers refused to do, saying that they must take the value out in rifles. Indignant at the loss of their money, it is not to be wondered at that, taking matters into their own hands, they should invade Persian Mekran in force, breathing threats of violence to all and sundry who should oppose their progress, intent on bringing the nakhudas to reason, and with the avowed intention of cutting the telegraph-line and of driving the "kafir" into the sea. Any chance there may at one time have been of Mir Barkat—who periodically used to apply for an increase in the already liberal allowance granted him for the protection of the line—coming in, vanished with the news that the Afghans were about to place themselves under his leadership. It looked as if the wave of indignation which had swept over the North-West Frontier in October, and spent itself in impotent fury along the Afridi border, were now about to break again on the low sandy shores of Persian Mekran.

CHAPTER XI

THE DASH ON BINT

"The ubiquitous tendency to territorial expansion, which is so marked a feature in European States of the period, results in a corresponding contraction of the ground free equally to all; and as this narrows there cannot but be increasing jealousy of every movement which carries with it a threat of exclusive control, whether by acquisition or by predominant influence, especially if the latter depend, not on fair commercial struggle in open markets, but upon the alien elements of military and political force."—CAPTAIN MAHAN: *Problems of Asia.*

IT was not till March 30 that it was known that the Government had decided to send an expedition against these invaders of Persian territory. News had, indeed, been received that a small telephone-hut somewhere between Jask and Chahbar had been wrecked, and the telephone clerk forced to fly for his life. But beyond this nothing further, as far as it was known, had happened, although the Afghans had by this time moved down by easy stages towards the coast, and were occupying a line of country just south of Bint (a town midway between Bampur and the coast) stretching away westward towards Bashakard and Biyaban.

The reluctance of the Government to send an

expedition to Mekran may possibly be attributed to the anxious jealousy with which any forward movement on our part in Southern Persia is looked upon by Russia and Germany, the former because she has interests there herself, and the latter because she has none. This feeling of jealousy is admirably appreciated in the quotation from Mahan's "Problems of Asia" which I have placed at the head of this chapter. The secrecy with which preparations were made and the operations conducted was commented on in the following words by Mr. Lovat Fraser in a paper on "Gun-running in the Persian Gulf," read by him before the Central Asian Society on May 17.

"You cannot mobilize a squadron and an expeditionary force and start out to conduct warlike operations, and then ask the rest of the world to be kind enough to look the other way."

The apparent leisureliness of the movements of the Afghans, and the fact that, with the single exception of the molestation of an isolated line-guard, no outrage had been committed, could not be taken as an indication that their warlike temper had been exaggerated. Their very numbers served to negative such an assumption. Moreover, small accessions to the Ghilzai host continued to make their appearance. The circumstance that the departure of the main body from Afghanistan had been known as early as in October, 1910, and the fact that they had frequently halted for weeks at a time in places where good pasture was available was held by many to be a sign of their deliberate intention to procure rifles at all costs, the more so since the month of May is the last in which it is possible to return over the waterless desert which now lay between them and the Afghan frontier. Only the year before the returning arms-caravans had suffered the most terrible privations and unmentionable hardships through having postponed till too late their return journey.

Realizing at last that the Ghilzais had in fact "come to stay," the Government on March 30 issued orders for the mobilization of a small force to proceed to the coast of Mekran, under the command of Rear-Admiral Sir Edmund Slade, K.C.I.E., Commander-in-Chief of the East Indies Squadron. The landing force was to be under the command of Colonel Delamain, D.S.O., 123rd Outram's Rifles, who had led a similar expedition up the Gulf the previous year, and consisted of the 104th Wellesley's Rifles, with two machine-guns, under the command of Major A. P. Stuart; the 32nd Mountain Battery, under Major Williamson Oswald; the 19th Company Sappers and Miners, and two sections of Field Ambulance—in all about 1,000 men.

On April 6 the naval Commander-in-Chief transferred his flag from H.M.S. *Hyacinth* to H.M.S. *Highflyer*, which had arrived two days before from England, and on April 7 the transports *Hardinge* and *Northbrook*, escorted by the *Highflyer*, steamed out of Bombay Harbour. As we

A "BOAT-CRUISER.'

COLONEL W. S. DELAMAIN AND STAFF.

passed the old flagship, flying her paying-off pennon, her gallant crew, who had borne the burden and heat of the day, and were now to return to England, gave us three cheers, which came faintly to us over the water.

The heat in Bombay had been pretty bad, but it was nothing compared to the stifling air between-decks. Both transports were packed to overflowing with men, mules, stores, and kit. The mules, of which there were about 230 on either ship, were stabled along both rails of the main deck, while the sepoys occupied the forecastle and the lower boat-deck. Shortly after starting we were startled by a furious trampling of hoofs on the deck, accompanied by the curious vocal noise of the mules, which is a cross between a neigh and a bray. Investigation resulted in the rescue of a sheep which had got under the hoofs of a mule, and but for timely succour would in a little time have been trampled to death. The removal of the sheep produced a monotonous void in the mules' daily round, until it was discovered that the wood of which the stalls were built was saturated with the most excellent salt. From that date onward "crib-chewing" became a favourite occupation, and by the time the expedition reached Bombay once again the mules must have been in debt to the Government of India for a considerable amount on the score of dilapidations.

On the fourth day after leaving Bombay a narrow yellow line bounded the horizon to the north. The coast between Chahbar and Jask affords but an open anchorage, and consists of a low, sandy, surf-beaten shore, backed a short distance inland by a series of difficult parallel mountain ranges running in a general direction north-west to south-east. Behind these we suspected that the Ghilzais were encamped. The villages along this coast are all well-known landing-places of the gun-runners—Gabrig, Sadaich, Rapch, Galag—the last of which was given out as our landing-place. It is situated about one mile up the eastern branch of the Rapch River, just inside an inconvenient bar. This river is one of the few perennial rivers along this coast.

At ten o'clock on the morning of Monday, April 10, the *Highflyer* and the *Northbrook* dropped anchor off the mouth of the Rapch between two and three miles from the shore, and the latter began immediately to disembark troops. It was some time before the *Hardinge* arrived, as she had dropped some distance behind owing to the fact that she was burning "country coal"—*i.e.*, Indian coal. A pilot launch was sent off to discover the best place for landing at that state of the tide, and on the way to the shore fell in with a patrolling "boat-cruiser," whose hirsute occupants, Ulyssean in aspect, hailed the boat with offers of assistance in finding the channel. The tide being at that hour somewhat low, it was found impossible to cross the bar, and so the landing had to be effected slightly to the eastward of the mouth. Hour after hour the launches came and went, each with its "tow" of three ship's lifeboats, until by three in the afternoon the *Northbrook's* complement formed up on the beach, and marched off to camp at the date-grove at Galag, one mile inland. The *Hardinge* had not been so lucky, for a stiff breeze springing up in the afternoon interrupted the landing, which was not completed until the following morning. The mules were landed in lifeboats from which the thwarts had been removed. On arrival in shore a cordon of sepoys was formed round the boat, from which the mules leapt into the water. The mules, on gaining terra-firma, were allowed one long roll in the sand, to take off the stiffness of their cramped positions on board—a diversion which they appeared thoroughly to enjoy—and were then loaded up preparatory to marching. The landing costume of the men, as may be seen in the photograph, was of the scantiest description; and very necessary it was, too, since the boats could rarely approach within seventy yards of the shore. The *Highflyer* also landed a contingent of Marines under Major Herriot, R.M.L.I.—handy men, every one of them, and already well versed in "Gulf lore." Blankets and "grub" were scarce that night at Galag, and most of us slept as we were on the sand.

The next day a tiring march in the heat of the day through a scrub desert brought the vanguard to a well, surrounded by an iron fence, from which all drank greedily, regardless of filters, and by evening the whole force was encamped about twelve miles inland at the telephone-hut at Rapch, the scene of the murder in 1897 by Baluchis of Mr. E. Graves, one of the Indo-European Telegraph Company's superintendents. Here the column was met by Sirdar Saiyid Khan of Geh, a semi-independent chief whose authority extends over the greater portion of Persian Mekran, a man with whom our relations have been on a friendly footing for some years past on account of the telegraph-line which traverses his territory, for the protection of which he receives a small subsidy.

At Galag the column had been met by Mr. E. G. Gregson, who had succeeded Colonel Malleson on special intelligence duty in the Persian Gulf in 1909, and whose intimate knowledge of all frontier questions, and personal acquaintance with the principal characters, notorious and otherwise, in gun-running circles, fitted him in a peculiar manner to accompany the expedition in the capacity of Political Officer. In a conversation with the latter and with Captain Craufurd, D.S.O., Gordon Highlanders, Intelligence Officer at Jask, the Sirdar readily agreed to lend his good offices on our behalf in inducing Sirdar Islam Khan of Bint to co-operate with us in the extinction of the arms traffic by excluding Afghans from his country. A letter in this sense was accordingly despatched to Sirdar Islam Khan, notifying him of the landing of the force, and requesting him, under the authority of the Persian Government, to come in, with the object of arriving at some solution of the situation. This interview took place in the Sirdar's camp at Rapch, where, under the shade of a giant tamarisk, a few rugs had been spread, on which the Sirdar reclined with his son. Two negro slaves handed cool water in a shallow brazen bowl, but out of our saddle-bags we produced some chocolate and a sparklet siphon, which surprised and delighted both father and son. Saiyid Khan in appearance is a man of fifty years of age, with the dark complexion of the true Baluch, and a melancholy expression in his dreamy eyes, which is accounted for by the fact that he is an opium-smoker. His son, a cheerful boy of ten or twelve years of age, rode with us several marches.

The experience of the previous day had convinced Colonel Delamain that the heat would not permit of day-marching, and henceforward all marching was done either by night or in the early morning. Except when night-marching, camp was therefore always broken before even the dawn was faintly perceptible in the eastern sky. At Rapch we were fortunate in obtaining about thirty camels after a slight palaver with their owners, who had driven them off into the scrub, thinking that they were to receive no payment for them. This settled, the column marched twelve miles to Chikai Bund on the Rapch River. Troops marched well, giving evidence of the exceptional mobility of the force, whose transport had been cut down to one blanket (4 pounds) for officers and half a blanket (2 pounds) for the men, no tents being allowed. The country traversed consisted at first of a tamarisk jungle, which later gave way to a gradual ascent over a stony plain, until the range of Zaur came into view. The route then dropped down once more into the bed of the Rapch River to the oasis of Chikai Bund on its left bank, about three miles from the entrance to the defile between Zaur and Chikai. Here a halt was made for three days, while mules were sent back to the coast for six days' extra rations. Up till now not a sign of life had been noticed. Except for deserted tracts of desert, surrounded by ditches, which appeared to have been subjected to a half-hearted attempted at cultivation, there was nothing that could have been termed a field. But as we entered the rich oasis of Chikai Bund, a herdsman was perceived driving off his cattle, and on the following day we caught a glimpse of a white-robed form high up on the opposite hillside, apparently scanning our position with interest. Karkindar lay now almost due west of us, and a short reconnaissance was made in this direction, in the hope of finding traces of the "dushman" (enemy), Karkindar being the home of Mullah Khair Mahommed, who was known to have collected a small following. Nothing came of it, however, beyond the establishment of helio communication with the coast.

On April 12 news arrived that Sirdar Islam Khan was already on his way down from Bint, in answer to the summons that had been addressed to him. On the following day one double company, under

SEPOYS LANDING THEIR KIT AT GALAG.

VIEW OF THE RAPCH RIVER AT CHIKAI BUND.

To face page 158.

the command of Major Williamson Oswald, with sappers and miners and one section of the Mountain Battery, moved through the Chikai defile and encamped about eight miles north of Chikai Bund, at Zamin, from which camp two cases of sniping were reported on the night of the 13th. Intelligence was now received from Biyaban that Mir Barkat had been active in instigating raids, and that many Ghilzais were moving through Bashakard into that province. The Khalifa Sahib was in Bampur, while the Ghilzais in Bint had retired through the gorge of Fanuch to Haimani, on the Bampur kafileh route.

The news of these dispositions made it finally clear that if any good were to result from this first landing, it was absolutely necessary that the column should reach Bint. With this intention it was gently broken to the Marines that they would be expected to furnish a camel corps, and a parade was ordered for the afternoon of Good Friday. Now, there is a good deal of difference between a riding-camel and a pack-camel, and those at the disposal of the Marines were chiefly of the latter variety, so that after the parade it became evident that if there were to be a camel corps at all, the Punjabis, who are accustomed to camels, and not the Marines, were the men to undertake the job. The Marines therefore magnanimously waived their claim to the honour, and were provided with mules.

With regard to camel transport, there can be no doubt of its superiority over all other in military operations in Persia. Owing to the rocky and impassable nature of the ground, mules are unable to undertake long days of successive marching with impunity. In addition to this, the camel is capable of carrying a load of 380 pounds to the mule's 160 pounds. Of this a smaller proportion is taken up by the animal's fodder, since the camel can practically exist on the scanty scrub of the desert, while in a waterless country its limit of endurance is greater than that of the mule.

As a means of locomotion he is by no means to be despised. There is something rhythmic and soothing in the ambling motion of this "grim, ungainly, gaunt, and ghastly" ship of the desert, as he pads along on silent foot through the "dasht," whether in the stifling glare of midday, in the silent watches of the night, or in the cool of the evening, with the sunset afterglow behind the hills and the fresh night breeze blowing up the pass. There is something restful when at the end of the day's march he sinks down in three ponderous movements, and begins to chew the cud, his jaws working alternately from right to left and from left to right. Now and again his long-lashed eye roams with a supercilious philosophy over the lines of mules, to whom the proximity of a camel, whether on account of its unpleasant odour or of its strange and terrifying appearance, furnishes a continual excuse for stampeding. The camel, indeed, seems to appear to the mule much as the Spanish horsemen appeared to the Peruvian aborigines, a new

CAMP AT CHIKAI BUND.

and undreamt-of monster. And, to be sure, he is. The interior of the camel is constructed on the latest and most scientific basis, and is the last word in desert economy. In addition to the ordinary furniture of the ruminating orders, he possesses auxiliary tanks for water and bunkers for fuel, and an emergency ration growing on his back. As a dog perspires only through his tongue, so the camel only perspires at the back of his neck, thus retaining the maximum of moisture in his body. Hence he will not stop and drink at every stream, as will a mule or a horse, if allowed, but will plod along all day, making his four to five miles an hour if a riding-camel, his two miles if a pack-animal.

Not only is he the symbol of the desert, but of the mysterious East. From Pekin to Kashgar and Yarkand the long caravans pass, accomplishing their journey in about six months. From Bokhara to the Indus extends another great camel route, and from Khorasan through Kerman to Bandar Abbas. The large Powindah tribe of the Ghilzais possesses at least 50,000 camels, beside which the 10,000 of the Queen of Sheba appears paltry and pretentious. The two-humped Bactrian camel of Central Asia is not considered such a good marcher as the Arabian camel, but is eminently fitted by his long hair for crossing snowy passes at great altitudes, such as the Bamian Pass over the Hindu Kush, due north of Kabul.

For the rest, the camel is a vain creature, loving

to be decked out with gaudy trappings and tassels of red and green, yet he can hardly be called a good-looking animal, except for his liquid eye and glossy "back hair."

Having awaited the return of the convoy from the coast, the remainder of the column moved up through the Chikai defile on April 15, accompanied by Sirdar Saiyid Khan, to Zamin. That evening Sirdar Islam Khan also arrived in camp. But it was not until the next day that the meeting between him and the officer commanding the force occurred, during the march northward from Zamin. At one point the route led across an elevated plateau, or "dand," of vast extent, stretching away to the distant mountains without a sign of vegetation, reminding one of Sven Hedin's description of the Chang Tang Desert of Tibet. Over this tableland the barbarian cavalcade which constituted Islam Khan's bodyguard careered at full gallop, the horsemen bending low in the saddle as they picked up stones from the ground, or standing up in their stirrups as they brandished their rifles in the air, their gaily coloured clothing, embroidered saddles, and bandoliers crammed with cartridges, completing a characteristic spectacle. Islam Khan himself is a man of about thirty-five years of age. His face, though indicating a certain doggedness of character, has a pleasing expression, his aquiline nose, black beard, and fiercely bristling moustaches, contributing to a decidedly distinguished appearance. He expressed his readiness to meet the wishes of the British Government, and showed but a momentary surprise on learning that Bint was to remain the objective in spite of his compliance. It is probable that neither he nor the Ghilzais, whom he had been entertaining at Bint, had any real belief in our intention or ability to reach that point, thinking, no doubt, that we should be satisfied with the assurances of friendship so cordially given by its ruler.

If this had been their hope, they were sadly disappointed. On Easter Day, April 16, camp was broken at 3.30 a.m., and a twelve-mile march made to the entrance to the Pass of Korandab. The going was very bad, deep sand alternating with stony gulches, while the river had to be forded many times. Arrived in camp, Colonel Delamain acquainted the Sirdar of his intention to push on to Bint, a distance of thirty miles, that same evening. Thus the final march to Bint was undertaken by night. At five in the afternoon a picked mounted column, made up of a detachment of Marines, a detachment of the 104th, and a half-section of the Mountain Battery on camels, moved out of camp and up the Pass of Korandab.* The remainder of the column was to move up through the pass on the following day, as a support in case the flying column should be attacked, as it was impossible to know whether all the Ghilzais had retired from Bint. The route lay for twelve miles through the pass.

* Korandab = "The Meeting of the Waters." A large area drains through the narrow defile.

Several ineffectual attempts to delay us were made by the Sirdar and his attendants, who at sundown ostentatiously dismounted and spread their prayer-carpets for the evening prayer. This, however, although repeated more than once, had no visible effect on the rapid progress of the column, and the devout Mahommedans were forced to gallop to catch up with us again. At eight o'clock a two hours' halt was made until the moon rose. The end of the pass was now reached, and leaving the river-bed, the force passed over a long and difficult kotal and down into the river-bed again. Here a five minutes' halt was made, during which most of us slept soundly for three or four minutes. From thence a long succession of narrow and rocky gulches wound in and out among the mountains, till at last the huge rock of Bint, rising some 700 feet from the plain in which it stands, appeared in the distance as a filmy veil of blue in the fresh morning sunlight. Bint was reached at 6.30 on the morning of the 17th. At the foot of the rock, under its north-eastern face, is situated the village, containing a population estimated by various travellers in the neighbourhood of 2,000 souls. A long "mach," or belt, of date-palms borders the river, partially concealing the village with its mud fort, and among these the column encamped at a distance of about one mile from the village. The country surrounding Bint is dotted with curious conical hills of shale, suggesting an oil formation. Traces of oil were also noticed in the Rapch River

SIRDAR ISLAM KHAN OF BINT.

THE ROCK OF BINT.

To face page 164.

at the southern debouchment of the Korandab Pass, and it is not improbable that oil exists in considerable quantities in the neighbourhood. Far away to the north-east could be made out the violet crests of the Band-i-Nilag and the Lashar Range, the principal watershed of the district.

After breakfast and a short rest, Islam Khan appeared, and invited us to the village, where he said he had prepared a small "tomasha" in our honour. Colonel Delamain, however, considered it inadvisable to avail ourselves of this invitation, in view of the fanatical temper of the Baluchis, whose revengeful feelings might be awakened by the most trivial incident, and lead, perhaps, to a disaster. We had perforce to content ourselves with the distant view of the mud-fort peeping out from among the date-palms. Since it was not my fortune to enter the village of Bint, I will here quote the description of it given by Floyer:

"Accordingly, the following morning we walked across the common, and, entering through a breach in a curious natural sandstone wall, climbed up some steep, narrow, and filthy streets, whose uses for progression were subordinate to their value as manure-beds. We had noticed every day donkeys passing into the town laden with kik-grass roots, and now found every nook and corner throughout the town spread deep with kik-grass and old rice-straw.

"The houses of Bint, Fanuch, Maskhutan, and other Baluch towns, are simply built in what resembles an English crew-yard, or yard for wintering cattle in, and the smell at some seasons must be fearful. The quantity of rice-straw lying about, the sparrows, and the substantial look of the well-thatched houses, give the place at the back the appearance of a very slovenly English homestead."

Evidently we did not miss much!

After a halt of eight and a half hours, the column set out on the return journey and second night march of thirty miles. One mule had to be left behind through foundering, and shortly after the start a camel fell and broke its leg, and had to be killed. The object of this rapid advance on Bint was to impress the Baluchis. It was thought that this rapid advance on Bint would have a salutary effect on the Sirdar by dispelling the delusion, under which he had been labouring, that Bint was invulnerable to a small force, based on the sea seventy miles away. It affords, indeed, a valuable illustration of the effective radius of a small mounted force, entirely dependent on itself for supplies, operating in a barren and almost waterless district, and with a transport limited to one-tenth of what had hitherto been considered the irreducible minimum.

After the rapid march on and retirement from Bint, in which, counting the twelve miles already accomplished on the morning of the 16th, seventy-three miles had been covered in forty-nine hours, the force arrived back at Chikai Bund at dawn of the 19th. A portion of the mules left for the coast the same evening, where they were embarked

CHAPTER XII

A BRUSH WITH THE GUN-RUNNERS

"In the land that lies beyond
Erzeroum and Trebizond
  Garden-girt his fortress stood;
Plundered khan or caravan,
Journeying north from Koordistan,
  Gave him wealth and wine and food."

LONGFELLOW.

THE satisfactory results accruing from the first landing of the Mekran Field Force partook more of the nature of a political victory than of a military, and may be looked upon as a distinct step towards a permanent solution of the arms question—at any rate, as far as the more easterly routes employed by the gun-runners are concerned. For of late, as has been mentioned, the gun-runners have shown an increasing preference for the coast of Biyaban, as affording greater chances of success in running a cargo, owing to the lesser distance of open sea that has to be crossed. This factor probably aided Islam Khan materially in his decision to come to terms with the Government of India, as his profits must have decreased considerably during the last year. And in its turn, too, Islam Khan's decision to "come in" no doubt accounts for the entire lack of resistance that was offered to the advance; for, with the exception of the two cases of sniping reported from Zamin on the night of April 13, the column did not come into touch with the enemy at any point.

But the success of the establishment of friendly relations with Islam Khan was also in a great measure due to the friendly offices of Sirdar Saiyid Khan of Geh, the paramount chief of Persian Mekran, who has not always been on the best of terms with his neighbour. Moreover, he had further cause for jealousy of his rival, in that, while Islam Khan was reaping a substantial profit from the arms traffic, he himself, in loyalty to the Government of India, from whom he receives a small subsidy for the care and protection of the telegraph-line, was unable to engage in the traffic, and was forced to sit by and watch the arming of the Baluch tribes on his northern boundaries with rifles which he might well fear might be used against him in a not very distant future. However, the fact that he recently appointed Islam Khan his "vakil" for the province of Karwan points to the burial of the hatchet, though there can be no doubt that in Islam Khan Saiyid Khan has, if not a successful rival during his lifetime, a probable successor to the overlordship of Persian Mekran. It is well known that the Baluchis have no love for the Persians, and have for years succeeded in evading payment of all revenue, in spite of the periodical expeditions sent to collect it by the Governor-General of Kerman, under whose nominal jurisdiction this district lies. To such an extent has this authority declined that it would be easy for a strong man to make himself master of the whole of Persian Mekran.

A similar situation prevails in Biyaban, where Mir Barkat Khan, having used his legitimate position as Governor of that province to consolidate and extend his influence, has now seceded from his allegiance to the Persian Government, carrying with him the sympathies of practically the whole of the population, with the exception of that portion under the immediate control of Mir Haji of Sikui. It was to this quarter that the efforts of the Mekran Field Force were now to be directed.

After the return from Bint and the re-embarkation at Galag, the Mekran Field Force proceeded to the coast of Biyaban, where a second landing was effected on April 24 at the small coast village of Sirik, which lies at the mouth of the Gaz River. On the way up from the Rapch River, the transports had touched at Jask, for the purpose of renewing the supply of camels, which journeyed thence overland to Sirik. Jask was found to be full of refugees from Biyaban, who had fled there to escape from the cruelties that Mir Barkat Khan, gun-runner, outlaw, and erstwhile Governor of Biyaban, had, with the assistance of his motley following of Tahirzai tribes-people from the coast villages, Bashakardis from the interior, and a sprinkling of Afghans, perpetrated on the unfortunate supporters of Mir Haji, the present Governor. The Kalantar of Sarzeh, so it was reported, had been burnt to death by the orders of Mir Barkat a few weeks before; Mir Kambar of Kuhistak, on returning from the Batineh Coast of Arabia, whither he had been to transact some business, had found his houses burnt to the ground, his property destroyed, and his cattle lifted. From all sides came the tale of rapine and bloodshed, of murder and robbery. Men had been beaten; women had been robbed of their ornaments; villages lay deserted by their terror-stricken inhabitants. Thus did Mir Barkat hope to make himself master of the situation, and pave the way to a veritable orgy of gun-running.

At Sirik news was received that Mir Barkat had retired from Sarzeh into the mountains, and that Saiyid Abdul Rahim, his second in command, had left Goshki and was preparing to join him. A number of Martini rifles were brought into camp by the orders of Mir Haji, with the information that they had been saved from the wreck of an Arab dhow that had run ashore in a westerly gale about a week before. These had, incidentally, nearly fallen into the hands of Mir Barkat, who had been surprised in the act of carrying them off inland. The rifles, though new, were in a very rusty condition, but what most attracted the attention was the fact that they had no stocks. This method of packing them has been recently adopted,

"PANCH MINIT KA HALT HAI" IN THE TANG-I-SARZEH.

ENTRANCE TO THE TANG-I-SARZEH.

To face page 172.

both on account of convenience in transport and because the different tribes to whom they are eventually sold in Afghanistan and on the North-West Frontier prefer to make the stocks themselves—some with and some without the metal butt-plate. Marching eastward along the course of the Gaz River, through the well-tended date-palm groves which here clothe the foot of the coast range, evening found the force encamped on April 26 in the neighbourhood of Sarzeh Fort, having safely negotiated the narrow Tang-i-Sarzeh, through which the Gaz River finds its way to the sea. This coast range is composed of a stiff blue clay, known as "shur," capped with limestone. From the seaward side it presents a jagged horizon of sharply denticulated peaks; on the landward it falls away in a precipitous drop to the level plain, a noticeable feature common to the succeeding ranges which back it inland.

Towards the middle of the plain the ground rises gently to the fort of Sarzeh, the scene of a fight between Mir Barkat and a British force, made up of a company of the 117th Mahrattas from Jask and a landing-party from the cruiser *Fox*, as recently as on Christmas Day last. Arriving early in the morning in search of a consignment of arms of which news had been received, they surprised the occupants of the fort, who incontinently fled. At the same time another party of Barkat's men fired on the landing-party, who promptly took refuge in the fort, whence they were enabled to drive off their foes, though during the retirement to the coast a spirited rearguard action was fought through the Sarzeh Pass.

Sarzeh Fort occupies a commanding site, standing four-square and facing south, the entrance being on that side. It would form an ideal place for a frontier military post, commanding as it does one of the principal caravan routes from Jask into Bashakard. It belongs nominally to the Governor of Biyaban, but, being in such close proximity to the mountains, it is more often occupied by Mir Barkat, since it forms a convenient refuge for gun-runners while awaiting the arrival of a cargo of arms. Unlike the majority of Baluch strongholds, there is no central ark or citadel, but in each angle of the walls is a tower, those on the western side being circular, while those on the eastern are square. In the north-eastern corner is the crumbling mud-tower set apart for the use of the chief, the tribesmen, it is presumed, sleeping on the ramparts, or, if no enemy is to be apprehended, among the camels in the open space below. Here a quarry-like excavation seems to point to an attempt having been made to level the ground, which slopes away sharply to the eastward. As in all Baluch forts, a well, dry at the time of my visit, has been sunk right through the mound on which the fort is built to a considerable depth. Close by the fort is a small mat-hut village, whose solitary inhabitant, an aged man, too old for the wars, cursed me volubly as I returned to camp.

SARZEH FORT.

SARZEH FORT.

To face page 174

From Sarzeh a short march brought the column to Gwaj, whence, as we arrived, a cloud of dust betokened a small party of cavalry moving off rapidly to the hills. Here we found Mir Haji and his attendants, who had preceded us, seated under a spreading thorn-tree, excitedly discussing the contents of several letters, which had apparently been delivered by the party whose dusty departure we had just witnessed. One of those letters was from no less a personage than Mir Barkat himself. In it he begged to be excused for his discourtesy in not having met the column in person on its disembarkation at Sirik, pleading in extenuation of this omission urgent business in the mountains. He added, however, that he yet hoped for a personal meeting in the Marak Gorge, where he intended making a stand. From the remaining letters it appeared that Mir Barkat, with a large following, had come down from Sahri-i-Gurg, in the Kuh-i-Biyaban, with the intention of holding the narrow gorge by which the Marak, a tributary of the Gaz, flows out at Gwaj into the Sarzeh Plain. A reconnaissance of the pass having accordingly been made, the enemy had been found to be occupying a line of sangars halfway between the Marak defile and the pass of Pashak, where the Marak, leaving the Sahri-i-Gurg, the "plain of the wolf," enters the Kuh-i-Biyaban.

On the morning of April 28, Colonel Delamain, D.S.O., commanding the expedition, ordered an advance with the intention of forcing the pass. A picket that had been posted on the top of a hill commanding a view of the Marak Gorge reported that the enemy had vacated their position of the previous day, retiring up the pass in the direction of Pashak. The column therefore advanced through the Marak Gorge, following the river, which wound tortuously in and out between high benches of gravel and limestone detritus, cemented together by the blue clay from the surrounding hills. For mile after mile the column forced its way through the deep sand which filled the bed of the shrunken stream, through which every now and again men and mules splashed, stopping to drink and to fill their water-bottles and "chargles" (canvas skins). The day was hot, and the heat was accentuated by the funnel-like defile, into which the sun shone at an almost vertical angle. There was still no sign of the enemy, and the sight of an oorial on the mountain-side seemed an evil omen for the day. "No oorial would remain there," men said, "if the pass were held." It was impossible to send flanking-parties along the crest of the hills on either side, on account of their inaccessibility and the numerous ravines which separated each peak from the next. But what could be done was done. The advanced guard sent out a line of scouts through the willow-scrub, and a convenient hill was picketed now and again. Suddenly a muffled shot was heard somewhere ahead, another, and then another. An orderly galloped back and reported that the enemy had been located in sangars round the next bend in the pass. The position had indeed been well chosen. At a bend in the pass, where the limestone cliffs rose sheer and smooth from the river-bed, the "dushman" was discovered, skilfully ensangared right across the narrow valley. The vanguard, under the command of Major Turton, 104th Rifles, immediately opened fire on the sangars, and with the support of the advanced guard guns, which opened fire at 800 yards four minutes after the first shot had been fired, held its position until the arrival of the main force. Then, under cover of the 32nd Mounted Battery, a general advance was made, and the enemy could be seen leaving their position and retiring in open order with the greatest coolness to another line of sangars. Each line was successively carried, while the intermittent "cough, cough" of the machine-guns followed the retreating force across the open spaces. Each shell from the ten-pounders as it burst on the hillside laid bare a conspicuous round bare patch of blue clay. Many burst right over the sangars, and though it was afterwards ascertained that several of the enemy had been killed, the survivors succeeded in carrying their dead off the field of battle. At last the end of the pass was reached, and the fugitives divided into two bodies, some seeking refuge in the direction of Sahri-i-Gurg, others in a more easterly direction. One prisoner was taken, carrying a Werndl rifle, who had been concealed by his friends in a deserted mat-hut, severely wounded in the leg.

On the principle of the Persian proverb, "A jackal of Mazanderan is not caught but by a dog of Mazanderan,"* the services of the body-guards of Mir Haji and Mir Kambar had been enlisted for the purpose of executing a turning movement on the left flank of Mir Barkat's position, and these were instrumental in continuing the pursuit of the vanquished gun-runners far over the plain. The action lasted from 9.18 till a little past noon, the casualties to the force amounting to three sepoys wounded, whilst the enemy, whose numbers were estimated at 200, lost eight killed and twenty-four wounded, as was afterwards learnt.†

It is probable that the enemy encountered at Pashak was little more than the advanced guard of Barkat's main body at Sahri-i-Gurg, though, had the defence been attended with better success, no doubt large reinforcements of Bashakardis would have rolled up from all quarters. Neither Mir Barkat nor his lieutenant, Saiyid Abdul Rahim, were present at the fight, though the probable effect on the *morale* of Mir Barkat's following may be judged from the losses sustained by the gun-runners, among whom were the son of Ghulam Husain, Chief of Afon (Ahavand), mortally

* "Shagal i Mazanderan nagirad juz sagi Mazanderani."

† News has just reached me (October 1, 1911) of the murder at Gwaj of one of the native guides employed by the Expedition in the Marak Gorge. Mir Barkat, who is probably responsible for this outrage, is said to be in the neighbourhood of Bandar Abbas, awaiting the beginning of the cold-weather gun-running season.

wounded, and the son, brother, and nephew of Karimdad, headman of the Tahirzai, among the slain, besides two of Mir Barkat's confidential "gholams," or Suaheli slaves. In the face of these casualties it is difficult to foresee whence Mir Barkat is to recruit his following in the future.

Thus it so happened that, with the exception of a diminutive following of Bashakardis under Ali Abbas, son of Ghulam Husain, the whole of the enemy's force consisted of members of the Tahirzai tribe, Barkat's own men. These, it must be admitted, fought with the greatest bravery and determination, particularly their leader, Ali Abbas, who formed a rather conspicuous mark in a red puggaree, and retired shot through both thighs. But though the Ghilzais, who during February were reported to have invaded Persian Mekran, were conspicuously absent from the fight, the fact that they did actually exist, though not in such numbers as was at first reported, has, at any rate, been substantiated, not only by those whose business it was to collect trustworthy information as to the whereabouts of gun-running caravans, but indirectly through the principal Baluch Sirdar implicated in the traffic, as well as by the personal experience of a Persian army advancing on Bampur. During the first phase of the operations, and while the column was still in Bint, intelligence was received from a trustworthy source that at the approach of the troops a body of Afghans had retired on Fanuch, where it had joined a large kafileh, consisting of 500 men and 1,000 camels. On arrival at Gwaj further information had been elicited, to the effect that Mir Barkat had received a letter from these Ghilzais, promising active support and bidding him on no account to make peace with the Sirkar, for they were making all haste to join him in the highlands of Bashakard. There can be little doubt that it was this knowledge that decided Mir Barkat to oppose the column in the pass at Pashak, though the sudden defection of the whole of the Bashakardi tribesmen, numbering some 2,000 rifles, consequent on the non-arrival of the Afghans, was a severe blow to his fortunes. This non-arrival is, however, sufficiently explained by the news of the despatch of a Persian army from Kerman, which met a hostile force in the neighbourhood of Bampur, and is reported to have suffered a severe defeat.

A further advance not coming within the scope of the operations, the force encamped on the enemy's position, returning the next day to Gwaj, thence to the coast, the main body embarking at Sirik on May 3 for Bombay, while a small column under Colonel Walton, 104th Rifles, who had rejoined his regiment from leave in England in time for the fight of April 28, proceeded southwards by way of Goshki, Bris, and Gwan, to embark on May 6 at Bunji. This movement was undertaken with the object of strengthening Mir Haji's hold over the outlying villages from which Mir Barkat's following had been drawn.

During the time that it remained on shore, the force was accompanied by Mir Haji, who, as Governor of Biyaban, in the absence of the Governor of the Gulf Ports, represented the Persian Government, and also by Mir Kambar of Kuhistak, both of whom had recently been the victims of Mir Barkat and his raiding Tahirzai. This latter chieftain presented a more truculent appearance than even the most villainous of his retainers. He was attired in a "coat of many colours" of the kind made in Bint, the embroidery of which, covering the whole garment, was of a very rich and elaborate nature. His modern rifle was decorated with silver bands round the barrel, while the stock was studded with plates of the same metal. Round his waist he wore a bandolier neatly ornamented with fine brass wire, into which had been thrust a curiously shaped silver dagger in the form of a cross, the blade being slightly curved and the hilt set with a large turquoise. On this belt he carried a silver cartridge-box, of Shiraz workmanship, in the lid of which had been set a cornelian. But what lent him such a ferocious aspect were the crafty eyes, twinkling out from under bushy eyebrows and an enormous white turban; the bristling moustache and henna-dyed beard, and the brown lungi loosely fastened over his mouth and under his chin, to hide a throat-wound which he had received a short time before in an encounter with Mir Barkat's gang. As for Mir Haji, not only is Barkat Khan his son-in-law, rival, and predecessor in the governorship of Biyaban, but had it not been for the latter's active participation in the arms traffic, and his consequent outlawry by the Persian Government, there was small chance of his ever rising to the position which he now occupies. It was therefore with something more than mere zeal for law and order that Mir Haji suggested, and his and Mir Kambar's followers carried out, the successful turning movement of the 28th. The impression, however, created in his favour by the presence of the troops in Biyaban should suffice to establish his unchallenged supremacy in the district of which he is now "Zabt," or Governor. Incidentally we thereby gain an additional guarantee of a material reduction in the arms traffic at this point, since it would be virtually impossible for the nakhudas to run a cargo of rifles over from the new depot at Sohar without the fact coming to his knowledge.

It may be of interest to mention the fact that among the empty cartridge-cases found in the Baluch trenches after the action of the 28th, besides those of the principal Continental manufacturing States, were many of English make, specimens of which I retained as souvenirs.

The questions that were asked in Parliament by Colonel Yate, shortly after the return of the Mekran Expedition (May 1911), with regard to measures being taken for the protection of the Central Persian Telegraph-Line, raised another aspect of the point which originated in the British

MIR HAJI OF SIKUI, GOVERNOR OF BIYABAN, AND HIS COURT.

MIR KAMBAR OF KUHISTAK, WITH HIS SON AND TWO FOLLOWERS.

To face page 182.

note to Persia of October, 1910, to the effect that if the Persian Government should prove incapable of preserving order on the Southern Persian trade-routes, it would devolve on the British Government to put forward more effective measures for the purpose of safeguarding the interests of our own commerce in particular and that of foreign nations in general in the disturbed areas. The telegraph-line in question, after leaving Kerman, crosses the Dasht-i-Lut by way of Bam to Kuh-i-Malik Siah, where it enters British territory at Robat. Between Bam and the British frontier it intersects at more than one point with the caravan routes from Mekran and Biyaban, by which the returning arms caravans regain the Valley of the Helmund. What more likely than that, having been driven out empty-handed from Mekran, the Ghilzais should take what revenge lay in their power and destroy a few miles of telegraph-line? Only last year about four miles of wire were cut up by a party returning to Afghanistan, and carried away bodily to Ghazni, where it commanded a ready sale as a substitute for string in tying together the component parts of the Afghan plough. Fortunately, up to date the telegraph-line has remained intact. The point at issue, however, was not whether a force should have been moved out, presumably from Robat, to protect the line, since this was precluded by the approach of the hot weather and the consequent drying up of the water-supply, which makes it impossible for a column to operate in this district after a certain date. The real question, which still remains to be decided, is to what extent we are justified in interfering in Persia, and in taking our own precautions to insure that the concessions that have been granted to British subjects are not rendered nugatory by the inability of the Persian Government to provide any guarantees of proper protection; that our telegraphic communications with India are not in jeopardy from casual bands of disaffected tribes-people from a neighbouring State; and that effect is given to the assurances of the Persian Government, who profess to be in sympathy with our attempts to prevent the arming of hostile tribes on our North-West Frontier.

In this connection it is interesting to learn how the matter is regarded in the country through which the Mekran Field Force passed. Mir Haji, the chief whose authority has just been restored over the province of which he is Governor, professed himself anxious to learn when the British Government proposed carrying out their expressed intention of policing the trade-routes of Southern Persia, adding that the three months granted as respite to the Persian Government had long since run their course, and that the disturbing news from Bushire at that time (April-May) warranted the adoption of precautionary measures of the nature suggested. He was thinking, no doubt, of his own lands and of those of Mir Kambar of Kuhistak, so recently harried by Mir Barkat and his freebooters from a safe retreat in the fastnesses of Bashakard.

That there is no love lost between Persians and Baluchis is a truth on which it is needless to dwell. Persia fulfils no duty towards its province of Baluchistan, beyond the self-imposed task of extorting from time to time by force of arms what revenue can be squeezed out of the unlucky inhabitants. If we should be justified in policing the trade-routes of Southern Persia proper, surely, then, it is our duty to preserve the peace in Baluchistan, where a country, potentially fertile, as I shall attempt to show in the next chapter, is being kept back through the oppression of the Persians on the one hand, and the lawlessness of the neighbouring hill-tribes on the other.

CHAPTER XIII

THE FUTURE OF MEKRAN

"Before my dreamy eye
Stretches the desert with its shifting sands
And unimpeded sky."

LONGFELLOW.

WHILE interest still lingers over a country that has just been traversed by a British force, and which has hitherto remained to all intents and purposes a *terra incognita* even to the pioneers of British trade, it may not be out of place to offer a few remarks on the resources and possibilities of Persian Mekran, as far as it is possible to judge of them during a short and transitory visit. The probability, also, of a railway being constructed through Southern Persia in the not very distant future affords an additional reason for speculative interest in Mekran.

Of the early history of Mekran we can obtain only occasional glimpses, and for these are mainly indebted to the diligent researches of British officers who, such as Pottinger, Goldsmid, Holdich, and Sykes, have traversed this region in the service of their country; or to men such as Floyer, who, during a long residence in Mekran in the employment of the Indo-European Telegraph Company, explored the little-known interior of Persian Baluchistan, and gave to the world the results of his wanderings in "Unexplored Baluchistan." Such, indeed, is the isolation in which this out-of-the-way corner of Persia has been sunk for centuries that it is only when an Alexander, a Ghenghiz Khan, or a Nadir Shah, leads his victorious armies in this direction, that we gain more than the distorted and legendary accounts of mythical heroes or local chieftains handed down from mouth to mouth and sung by the gipsy bards* of Mekran. Since the time when Alexander led his army back from founding an empire on the Indus, almost every century has brought a fresh invasion, the Baluch Sirdars, then as now, yielding a minimum of homage to the conqueror of the moment. Persian dynasties and invaders from beyond—Sassanians, Hindus, Arabs from Aleppo; Saffars, Deilamis, Seljuks from Central Asia; Mongols and Afghans—each in turn have made themselves masters of Mekran, none, however, having been able to maintain more than a temporary supremacy over the hardy Baluch chieftains, in whom the spirit of patriotism, common to all hillmen, is so strongly implanted. In the majority of cases they were content to exact an exorbitant tribute at the time, and retire with a nominal title to the lands which they had conquered, but had been unable

* The Loris.

to retain. This is the position of Persia to-day with regard to Mekran.

As a result of these numerous irruptions of half-civilized tribes, the whole of Persian Baluchistan has been overlaid with successive deposits of ethnological sediment, differing in character according to the quarter from which they originated, much as the low-lying flats of the Kabul River around Peshawar differ in the character of their sediment according as to whether the Swat, the Bara, or the Kabul River was last in flood. These different tribes have, as a general rule, no very strongly marked territorial limitations, as among the Pathans, but are scattered broadcast throughout the country, their tribal occupation being a surer guide to their origin than the locality in which they are found. Much of this may be accounted for by their semi-nomadic habits. It must also be remembered that, besides the principal invasions to which allusion has already been made, there occurred many immigrations of which not the slightest historical records exist.

In most countries the original inhabitants, where yet they exist, are generally found in the course of ages to have sunk down in the scale, and to have been gradually forced into menial occupations by the races by whom they have been supplanted. This is true of Mekran, with one brilliant exception—namely, the Brahuis, an aboriginal tribe of Dravidian origin, according to Sykes, who have inhabited Mekran since the first dawn of history, and who yet in its more easterly districts have remained the dominant race. Among the remaining probably aboriginal tribes may be mentioned the mat-makers of Geh and Qasrkand, several nomadic tribes of graziers and camel-owners in the Jaghin and Sadaich Valleys, and the "Maids," or fishermen, who are almost certainly the descendants of the ancient "Ichthyophagi," or Fish-eaters, of whom Arrian speaks in his account of the voyage of Nearchus from the mouths of the Indus.

While landing at Galag, a good opportunity occurred of observing one of these "Maids" at work, fishing with a line some half a mile out to sea. At first sight, and from a distance, this ragged creature appeared to be standing motionless upon the face of the waters, but on a nearer approach he was seen to be supported on what looked like a mass of wreckage, through which the sea was breaking as it lay half submerged in the trough of the swell. This crazy craft is constructed of a framework of date-palm branches, ballasted with heavy blocks from the trunk of the same tree, and, in spite of its appearance of instability, is said to possess great buoyancy.

Of the tribes in Biyaban, the Mirs of Indian origin are found also in Mekran; the Shaikh are of Arab descent; the Hot constitute the family of the Mirs of Jask; and the Tahirzai, of whom I can find no previous mention, are agriculturists and inhabit the inner valleys of the coast district.

With the exception of the Brahuis in the east

of Mekran and the Gichki, descended from Rajput chiefs, the Baluch Sirdars are all descended from the large horde of Rinds that migrated from Aleppo early in the Mahommedan era. The principal of these families are the Nahruis of Geh, Bint, and Qasrkand; the Jadgals of Bir, Dashtiari, and Bahu; and the Hots of Jask and Biyaban. All the Baluch Sirdars are interrelated, and form a kind of feudal confederacy under Saiyid Khan of Geh, who, as paramount chief of Mekran, is nominally under the Deputy-Governor of Bampur, who, in turn, is responsible to the Governor-General of Kirman. It is this family relationship which enables the Baluch Sirdars to present such a determined front to any undue attempt on the part of the Persian Government to interfere in the affairs of Baluchistan, though among themselves there is a continual undercurrent of animosity and intrigue. For many years the Persian Government has confined itself to making periodical incursions in force into Baluchistan, for the purpose of collecting revenue; but whether the present army, which is reported to have been defeated in the neighbourhood of Bampur, was sent to drive out the gun-runners, or whether the opportunity of collecting revenue while the British troops were still in the country was considered too good to be lost, does not appear. At any rate, success does not seem to have attended its efforts.

Mekran is divided into the five districts of Jask, Geh, Qasrkand, Dashtiari, and Bahu, which, with the exception of the first, are under the Sirdar of Geh, and pay, or are supposed to pay, an annual tribute to the Persian Deputy-Governor of Bampur. The taxes are collected, but it is very doubtful whether the Governor of Bampur ever sees more than a portion of them. Jask, though reckoned a district of Mekran, is under the Daria Begi, or Governor of the Gulf Ports, of whom it is, however, almost entirely independent, paying no taxes. Biyaban also forms part of the province of the Gulf Ports, but the mountainous and inaccessible region of Bashakard, running down like a wedge between Mekran and Biyaban, is a subdistrict of Rudbar, a district of Kirman. It would be very much better were Bashakard incorporated either with Baluchistan or the Gulf Ports, for, lying at a considerable distance from, it is virtually independent of, Kirman, and, being infested with robbers, is a distinct menace, not only to the comparatively unimportant country to the south and south-east, but to the highly important trade-routes leading from Bandar Abbas to Kirman. Caravans are constantly being attacked and looted by these robbers from Bashakard, and being outside the jurisdiction of the Daria Begi, the latter cannot, while the Governor of Kirman will not, take any steps to put a stop to the nuisance.

Towns can hardly be said to exist in Mekran. Geh, Bint, and Qasrkand, are little more than large villages of 2,000 inhabitants, though Chahbar and Jask, on account of their European connection, might rank as such. Among the remaining villages may be mentioned Old Jask, the residence of the hereditary chiefs of Jask, wiped out by a rival Sirdar some years since; Grishkin, a port at the mouth of the Jaghin River, which carries on a not unimportant trade with the opposite coast of Arabia; Bir, a few miles west of Chahbar; and Tiz, a suburb of the latter port, which in early times was the centre of a large silk export from the Bampur region.

Our own relations with Persian Mekran have been chiefly in connection with the delimitation of the boundary between it and British Mekran, which was effected by the Goldsmid Mission by a line drawn from a point eight miles east of Gwatar to Kuhak, some hundred miles inland. It was this recognition of Persian interests in Mekran that incidentally suggested to her the idea of reasserting her rather shadowy authority over this turbulent district. Since that time two British expeditions have penetrated Mekran, one to avenge the murder of Mr. Graves in Karwan in 1897, and the second in 1902, under Major Tighe, as escort to Major Showers, Political Agent, Kalat, for the purpose of destroying some forts in the Sarhad district of Persian Baluchistan which were being used as strongholds whence raids might be committed into British territory.

As to commercial relations, these can hardly be said ever to have existed. It was at Jask in 1619 that British trade first sought to tap the markets of

Southern Persia. Here the East India Company had its first factory in the Gulf, whence in 1622 it was transferred to the port of Gombroon or Bandar Abbas, and the connection ceased.* In 1904-05 the itinerary at first selected for the Indian Commercial Mission to South-Eastern Persia included a return journey from Kirman by way of the fertile district of Bam-Narmashir, across the Gishu Pass, through the Bampur Valley and Persian Baluchistan (this would probably have included a visit to the districts of Geh, Bint and Qasrkand), to Magas; thence, via Kuhak and the Kej Valley, to the coast at Gwadur or Pasni. But on arrival in Persia "the tour through a sandy and stony land, which grudgingly supports a sparse population of wild and poverty-stricken nomads," where there was "no trade worth speaking of, nor any hope of increasing it," was ultimately abandoned.† Thus for the second time British trade passed by on the other side.

From the foregoing sketch it will be seen that the drawbacks that have beset Persian Baluchistan in the past—the scanty population, the huge uncultivated areas—have been due as much to the maladministration and extortion of the succeeding conquerors who from time to time have imposed their will on the wretched population as to the vagaries of an unkindly Nature.

It would be premature to attempt to forecast

* Curzon's "Persia."

† Report on the Mission.

the actual route that a railway through Southern Persia would follow, but this much may possibly be hazarded with safety, that such a railway, if built, will pass through Persian Baluchistan, and connect with the Indian system, not at Quetta, as might be expected, but at Karachi. The difficult gradients in the neighbourhood of Nushki, and the desert zone which lies across the path of the more northerly route, combine to favour the idea that the more southerly, across Persian Baluchistan, will eventually be adopted. It is possible that to many the idea of developing Mekran will appear in the light of making a silk purse out of a sow's ear. I do not wish to claim too much for Mekran—*qui trop embrace, mal étreint*—but in the construction of a railway it is necessary to take into account the material resources of the district through which it is to pass, and although no glowing future can be predicted for Mekran, as has been for other parts of the Shah's dominions—at least, for many a long year to come—yet, it is capable of sufficient development to provide valuable feeders for the trunk line.

In order to make the position clear it will be necessary to give a rather detailed account of the orographical features of the country, in which, for the sake of homogeneity, it is proposed to include, under the geographical expression "Mekran," all that country lying to the south of the latitude of Bandar Abbas as far as the British frontier, and including the subdistricts of Biyaban and Bashakard, belonging respectively to the provinces of the Gulf Ports and of Kirman.

Geographically speaking, Mekran may be divided into three distinct belts, of which the most southerly consists of a broad strip of alluvial country extending on an average some ten to fifteen miles inland to the foot of the coast range. In Mekran proper this coast range is composed of a sandy conglomerate of gravel and shells, while in Biyaban it is formed of the stiff blue clay known as "shur," capped with sloping strata of white limestone several feet in thickness. From the seaward side it presents a jagged horizon of sharply denticulated peaks; on the landward it falls away in a precipitous drop to the level plain—a feature common to the succeeding ranges which back it inland. At the foot of this range, where it approaches the shore, are low-lying mangrove swamps and long stretches of driven sand, while in places are to be found groves of date-palms, villages, and scanty cultivation.

While in Biyaban I had the opportunity of visiting the Governor of Biyaban in his mud fort at Sirik, and of obtaining a nearer view of one of these coast villages. Sirik lies about three miles from the shore, from which it is concealed to view by a long line of carefully tended palm-trees. The village consists of some scores of huts made of date-palm branches, and thatched with the leaves of the dwarf "pish" palm, clustering round the square mud fort in the centre, while to the left is a large banked-up reservoir. As we entered the village women were passing to and fro carrying pitchers of water on their heads, but these soon disappeared into the huts, modestly drawing the corner of their veils across their faces. It is impossible to describe the impression of squalor and poverty that the first sight of these rude dwellings produces on one. Unventilated and unlit but by the narrow entrance, the furniture of these hovels rarely runs to anything more luxurious than a threadbare Bashakardi carpet, a long red bolster slip filled with hay, a few copper cooking-pots, a cracked looking-glass, a bag of beads from the Somali coast, some baskets of dates, a saddle-bag or two, and a naked boy, while in the corner may be seen an old matchlock "jezail," and hanging on the walls the pendant camel's-hair trappings which lend to the ungainly "shutar" (camel) such an air of superiority.

Entering the mud fort through a kind of guard-house, where a malefactor was undergoing punishment in the stocks, we came upon an open court, in the middle of which was an empty mud tank and a small heap of grain, which some woman had no doubt been engaged in winnowing when our appearance put her to flight. To right and left were low and gloomy doorways leading to dark recesses, while in front, under a high portico, supported by cylindrical pillars of uncommon thickness, sat the Governor, on a rich carpet, surrounded by his advisers, retainers, and negro slaves, passing from hand to hand the gurgling "kalyan."

Behind the coast range is an intermediate belt composed of parallel ranges of hills of no great height, and valleys, uninhabited for the most part, but possessing a light clay soil, which supports a few oases of date-palms and a luxurious growth of tamarisk and acacia, camel-thorn and "akh," while hay, dwarf melons, wild indigo, and wild-flowers, abound after the rains. The oasis of Chikai Bund, at which the force encamped on the march up to Bint, and also on the way back, for several days, provided a plentiful supply of first-class hay, and all along the banks of the Rapch at this point the vegetation was especially luxuriant.

Behind this intermediate belt the country rises again through a third zone of rugged mountains, stark and riven plateaux, ravines choked with boulders, to the distant Lashar Range, which, extending westward as the Band-i-Nushki to its right-angled junction with the Band-i-Marz, or mountains of Bashakard, eastward as the Band-i-Nilag to the British frontier, forms the water-parting between the basins of the Gulf of Oman and the Jaz Morian Hamun—the last remnant of an inland sea probably still existent in early historical times.

There is no reason to suppose that Mekran is any less fertile than any other part of Persia. Given better government and the abolition of the pernicious system of farming the taxes—"pishkesh" (the "graft" of America)—and other methods of extortion, a largely increased area might speedily be brought into cultivation—an act of enterprise which the humble tiller of the soil has hitherto refrained from committing through fear of increased taxation. To those who have seen "in the rough" the type of country which in Western America, despised at first even by the cattle-rancher, has become the richest fruit lands in the world, or to those who are acquainted with the gigantic schemes that are in hand for the irrigation of Mesopotamia, of Upper Egypt, and of the Sind "desert," the latter of which reproduces in many striking ways the characteristics of Mekran, the problem of effecting the metamorphosis of Mekran would not present such apparently insuperable difficulties.

The water-supply of Mekran, as obtained from the perennial rivers—*i.e.*, those that take their source in the main watershed—is both excellent and abundant. From the Rudkhaneh-i-Minab, the classical Anamis, where Nearchus brought his celebrated voyage to a close, to the Bay of Gwatar, there are no fewer than ten such rivers, all of which have quite respectable tributaries. As waterways they are, of course, valueless, being seldom more than 18 inches deep, and never continually so, except perhaps in the flood season. The most important of these flow into the Gulf of Oman —namely, the Jaghin, the Sadaich, the Rapch, the Geh, and the combined course of the Dashtiari and Bahu Rivers. Between them are many smaller streams, rising mostly in the middle belt, which dry up altogether in the hot weather, and whose waters are brackish and generally unfit to drink, even for beasts. The rivers of Biyaban, the Mazavi and the Gaz, also rise in the main range, but are shorter, and flow into the Straits of Hormuz, carrying with them quantities of gypsum, held in suspension and obtained from the limestone formation, which, together with the "shur" or stiff blue clay, is everywhere to be seen, the latter rising in jagged cliffs, seamed with myriads of tiny perpendicular runnels and scoriations. The Marak River, a tributary of the Gaz, where it forces its way through the gorge between the plains of Sahra-i-Gurg and Sarzeh, has formed on the inner side of the bends in its course high benches of this mixture of limestone and clay soil, which appears to possess a greater fertility than the alluvial soil of Mekran proper. At any rate, the cultivation here is in a more advanced condition, the general aspect of Biyaban being somewhat in the nature of a surprise to eyes accustomed to the dreary wastes of uncultivated plain that had been encountered during the advance up the Valley of the Rapch. On all sides waving fields of wheat and barley stretched away to the distant curtain-wall of limestone, while the landscape was filled in by a profusion of tamarisk, mimosa, and acacia, with the usual date-groves, and an occasional field of "jowari" (millet) and lucerne. It was by far the most fertile part we had yet traversed in this land, where the evil administration of the Persian Government, the rapacity of the tax-farmer, and the ever-present menace of the robber hillmen, have combined to atrophy the agricultural instinct in the oppressed and down-trodden peasantry. It is only necessary to mention that these crops have been produced by the simple rainfall of the district to realize what might be achieved were proper steps taken to store the water, which comes down in such quantities from the hills, for the purposes of irrigation.

For many years it was thought that the Bampur River drained out into the Gulf of Oman, but this mistake has been explained now by the fact that the principal rivers of Mekran proper rise on the northern slopes of the Lashar Range, and, hemmed in by a kind of "trans-Lashar Range," bend southwards, boring their way through wild and fantastic gorge scenery, that has more than once inspired the pen of the traveller. During and just after the rains, which occur in December and January (Mekran being outside the monsoon area), these gorges are filled with raging torrents, by which many a caravan has been engulfed while making an ill-judged attempt to negotiate the passes. Lower down they inundate the whole of the coast district, sometimes rendering impassable for many days at a time the Rah-i-Daria, or coast road, which runs at a distance of ten miles or so inland, connecting the Mekran ports of Gwatar, Chahbar, and Jask. It is along this road that the Indo-European telegraph land-line runs to Jask, and it is also at the intersection of this road with the courses of the rivers that the more important coast villages are situated. But for the vernal floods these villages would in all probability not exist, as they are mostly uninhabitable and deserted in the hot weather.

The existence of these rocky gorges tends to simplify in a great degree the problem of water-storage, and renders the country in many parts peculiarly adapted for successful irrigation. Nature has, indeed, herself supplied an object-lesson in this direction by the vertical uptilting of the limestone strata, which, acting as a natural dam, serve to retain in deep and limpid pools far up among the mountains the residue of the rains, which at present, neglected by the unthrifty inhabitant of the plain, flow to waste in the sandy nala-beds of the coast district. All over the Middle East are to be found the remains of irrigation works, some of them on a vast scale, and one cannot doubt that the noble cities and fertile gardens of ancient Persia were entirely dependent on the maintenance of such dams as that on the Halil Rud, a little above the city of Jiruft, destroyed probably at the time of the downfall of the Seljuk Dynasty, but even to-day capable of being sufficiently restored to hold a large quantity of water.*

Immense reservoirs of this kind might easily be constructed at comparatively small cost among the hills, where the narrow gorges and oval-shaped

* Sykes.

valleys permit, and if these were not needed, smaller dams would suffice to raise the river-levels high enough to admit of the water being led off into irrigation channels. At present there is no system of irrigation worthy the name beyond the "bund" round the date-grove, not even the homely and primitive "kariz," "qanat," or covered ditch.

The principal industries and occupations carried on by the inhabitants of Mekran are camel-breeding, mat-making, fishing, and, in a minor degree, agriculture and grazing, and from these practically all the trade is formed. The principal camel-breeding centres are at Geh and in the Rapch, Sadaich, and Jaghin Valleys. A considerable export trade is carried on in dried fish with Maskat, forming one of the principal means of livelihood for the poverty-stricken coast population. With the dried-fish industry may be mentioned the export of sharks' fins and isinglass, also to Maskat, thence to China and the East, where they are valued partly as delicacies and partly for their medicinal properties. Next to the fishing industry that of mat-making ranks perhaps in importance, being carried on wherever the dwarf palm exists. Other occupations are those of carpet-making in Jask and Bashakard, a black-and-white carpet known as "khirsak" being peculiar to the Jask district. In Bint a curious kind of embroidered coat, worn by all the notables of Persian Băluchistan, is made. The embroidery on these coats is of a very high order, resembling in pattern and effect the richness of a Persian carpet in miniature. In a country where so much has remained unchanged since early Biblical times—the legend of Jonah is said to have originated on the shores of an inland sea that existed here formerly—it would hardly be surprising were this coat the lineal descendant of the original "coat of many colours" that excited the envy of Joseph's brethren. The more usual crops raised include wheat and barley in spring; dates and jowari in autumn; small quantities of rice and cotton are also grown. Live-stock is confined to a few herds of humped cattle of a breed peculiar to the country, and a few flocks of "dumba" (fat-tailed sheep) and goats. Camels and donkeys are the beasts of burden.

With this meagre stock-in-trade it is not to be wondered at that European trade has impatiently gone elsewhere. As far as inland communications are concerned, Mekran is no worse off than other parts of Southern Persia. The principal caravan routes connecting the coast with the interior follow the course of the rivers. The most important of these is undoubtedly that which from Chahbar strikes inland up the valley of the Dashtiari River past Qasrkand, over a low kotal, and down into the valley of the Bampur River. At Bampur it connects with the main caravan route to Kirman via Bam and Rayin, and also with the Sistan-Khorasan route through Robat and Nasratabad. Next in importance is that connecting Jask with the first, by way of the Sadaich River Valley and Bint. Other routes ascend the Jaghin and the Rapch, the former, as already mentioned, being a favourite with gun-runners.

One of the most debilitating disadvantages with which the trade of Mekran has to contend with at the present day is the total absence of any suitable ports along its coasts capable of accommodating ships of even such moderate draught as those employed in the Gulf. At Gwatar, Chahbar, and Jask, the two last of which are regular places of call for the British India Line, vessels have to anchor as much as three or four miles from the shore, and discharging a cargo is rendered difficult by the surf, and by the ever-present possibility of the dangerous "shumal" springing up at any moment. In early times, Chahbar—or rather Tiz, as it then was—boasted a considerable trade in silk, coming down from the interior by way of the Bampur-Chahbar caravan route. The possibility of ever revivifying this route as an alternative artery of trade for the more easterly portions of the commercial catchment-basin of Bandar Abbas depends on the development of the country that lies between Bampur and Chahbar. At present the trade of Chahbar is slightly on the decline, owing possibly to the rapid development of Bandar Abbas and amounts to about two lakhs and a half of rupees per annum, of which one lakh accounts for imports; while that of Gwatar amounts to one lakh, of which a third is in imported goods. Imports consist of Manchester cotton goods, rice, flour, lead, iron, tobacco, beads, oil, matches, tea, thread, silk, spices, and sugar, for which latter commodity there is said to be an ever-increasing demand in Persia.

It is improbable that Jask will ever rise above its present position, overshadowed as it is on one side by Bandar Abbas, and on the other by Chahbar. It has no commercial hinterland worth mentioning, while that of Chahbar already includes Geh, Bint, Qasr-kand, Fanuch, Bampur, and Fehruj, and there is no reason why it should not be extended so as to embrace Sarhad and Saravan, when developed, and Sistan and Bam-Narmashir, for which, however, it will have to compete with Bandar Abbas.

In his valuable report on the Indian Commercial Mission to South-Eastern Persia, Mr. Newcomen, its president, pointed out that the value of our trade with Persia lay in the fact that we were able to supply her with articles which she was unable to produce herself, whilst taking from her raw materials, chiefly of a costly nature, such as gums, drugs, spices, and dye-stuffs. He also drew attention to the fact that Persia is not yet sufficiently developed to produce enough raw material to pay for the value of her imports. This makes it quite clear that before Persian Mekran can be made a profitable field for commerce her purchasing power must be increased by the full development of her internal resources. "Pish" palm mats, dates, and dried fish, will not buy the commodities of the West, for which all over Persia there is an ever-increasing demand, and in order to produce this purchasing power it will be necessary for the husbandmen of Mekran to import and cultivate the valuable plants of the gums, spices, and dye-stuffs, which already form such a large item in the material resources of the rich province of Kirman. Indigo already grows wild in Mekran. Henna, saffron, and madder, should follow it, and the valuable gum-tragacanth, asafœtida, and colocynth. For those plants that need moisture the coast district can provide up to 70 per cent. and 80 per cent. of atmospheric saturation. Long-staple cotton should grow well and compete successfully with the short-staple cotton of Khorasan, rice in the flooded coast-belt, and coffee where it is not subject to inundation, but where the water-laden sea air might yield results equal to those of far-famed Mokha. Inland the climate is dry and stimulating, and suitable for the production of cereals, and also for sheep-farming, on account of the saline characteristics of a great part of the soil.

The mineral resources of Mekran are probably very limited, although the fabled and mysterious mountain of "Kuh-i-Taftan" in the Saravan Highlands of Northern Persian Baluchistan is reputed to be rich in the precious as well as the useful metals. It is, however, not improbable that oil and sulphur exist in workable quantities, especially as Mekran lies in the Southern Persian oil-belt, which stretches more or less from the Karun River to the Afghan "Garmsir." An oil formation certainly exists in the vicinity of Bint, and traces of sulphur were distinctly noticeable in the water of the Gaz River in Biyaban.

Such, indeed, as I have described them, I believe to be the resources and possibilities of Persian Mekran, but the future development of the country on economic lines rests with the Persian Government and with her advisers among the European nations, and unless the vampire of Persian official peculation prove too strong for the reborn spirit of Persian nationality—the latest child among the nations—it may well come to pass that the land, into which the Almighty is reputed by its inhabitants to have cast all the refuse left over from the creation of the world, may at length be reclaimed.

INDEX

27